# Meditation For Stress

*Using Silence To Soothe The Troubled Mind*

*With a forward by Dr K. Rubia, Professor of Cognitive Neuroscience at the Institute of Psychiatry, King's College, London, UK*

# Meditation For Stress

by Nigel Powell

All Rights Reserved
No part of this book may be reproduced or
transmitted by any means, electronic,
mechanical, photocopying or otherwise
without the prior permission of the
publisher

ISBN 978-0-9548519-1-0

Copyright © Corvalis Publishing 2014
London
www.corvalis.co.uk
www.meditationforstress.net

Dedicated to my Mother
*and with thanks to my beautiful wife*

*"Embrace uncertainty! Recognize its potential to deliver powerful positive change, and open up to it. Avoid the urge to retreat to safety and security, as it is a false paradise, a dark space within which the spirit withers. Life is for living!"*

# - CONTENTS -

Preface
Forward

Chapter One -
Introduction

Chapter Two -
Overview of Stress

Chapter Three -
The Stress Created By Our Noisy Environment

Chapter Four -
Meditation, Thoughts and The Mind

Chapter Five -
Meditation, Thoughts and the Physical Body

Chapter Six -
Introduction To Thoughtless Meditation

Chapter Seven -
The Three Step Meditation Program

Chapter Eight -
Practical Seven Week Exercises

Conclusion & Resources
Appendix   I -  Personal Balance Checklist
Appendix  II -  Meditation Tips
Appendix III -  Meditation To Improve Sleep
Appendix IV -  Test Your Stress Level
Appendix  V  -  An Hypothesis

## The Author

Nigel Powell is a freelance journalist for The Times and Sunday Times newspaper in London and is the author of the Sunday Times Book of Computer Answers published by Harper Collins. He has taught and organised yoga meditation classes and seminars around the world for over two decades, and is a regular supporter of community programmes run by the Sahaja Meditation charitable trust in the UK. He has an honours degree in law (LLB), a masters degree in business administration (MBA) and lives in West London.

# - PREFACE -

The mind's a funny old thing, isn't it? When I started writing this book I was in the middle of a rather difficult period in my life, having become a victim of the economic climate of the time. Hardly the right place or right time to start writing, I suspect you're thinking. And you're right, except for the fact that a good deal of the motivation for producing this book was created by those experiences.

And here I have to add a small confession. Having been a happy meditator for over 22 years, during which time I had hosted numerous seminars and written detailed courses on how to meditate, I was extremely surprised by how difficult it was to shake off the stressful feelings that come from unpleasant personal circumstances. My mind wasn't playing nicely, despite my regular daily meditation. It was as if the events I was facing were specifically designed to shake me out of my comfort zone and force me to look at my life, meditation practice and mental resilience in absolute detail.

After two decades of meditating, I have to confess that I had grown comfortable with my knowledge and with my practice. Confident that I could handle most events and stay balanced and calm. So imagine my surprise when I found that facing these problems with my small business threw me out of balance in a real and significant way. Having spent decades telling people how meditation will make you a calmer, more resilient personality, here I was suddenly faced with a situation which was causing me to lose my cool. How could that happen?

My solution was to go into emergency mode and dive even deeper into the practice of meditation which had served me so well for the previous 20 years. I made sure I did not miss any meditations, either in the morning or my second evening one before retiring to bed, and I deliberately left myself enough time to meditate long enough to gain the full benefit of every session. In effect I took the whole process of meditation much more seriously than ever before, without being fanatical, to ensure I had banished any signs of complacency.

My efforts lasted the good part of a year, and while I am happy to report that I never missed a minute of sleep over the situation, it was definitely a struggle to find the familiar sense of inner peace which suddenly seemed to have gone on an extended vacation. I was thinking far too much about stuff. But then, like a thirsty man cresting a dune to see the oasis, the peace of my meditations returned and I began to recover the calm enjoyment of life that I cherish. Worries about dwindling savings faded, as did the unease about an uncertain future.

So what did I learn from the experience? Well the key thing was that when things get rough, it is absolutely essential to continue with the meditation, because it WILL get you through the unsettled patch. Over the decades I've lost count of the number of times people have come up to me and said something like – "*sorry I couldn't attend classes for a few weeks, but there was a death in the family...*" or "*...I had some serious domestic problems to sort out...*" or similar sentiments.

It amazes me that people will stop meditating at the very time when they most need to soothe their troubled mental state, rather like telling a doctor, "*sorry I couldn't take your medicine this week because I was a wee bit ill.*" Very strange! In my case, I took action to reinforce my meditation practice immediately I noticed myself losing the sense of inner peace all those months back. I would make sure that I allowed enough time for the silence to manifest properly, and I would not short cut the process or allow my mental clutter to divert me from achieving the thoughtless state I needed every single day.

Which brings me back to this book. When I say the motivation for the book came from these experiences it's very true. Although it's also true to say that it was actually a very nice lady I met a while back at one of our weekly meditation classes who really pulled the trigger on the idea of a book combining meditation with stress relief. She had recently left her high powered job in the city and came to our meeting to try and lose her stress after finding it difficult to find a replacement job within a few months. With her mortgage ticking away and all that.

We talked at length via email as well as at the weekly meetings, so I knew what she was going through, even though my own situation hadn't really kicked in yet. And yet, the more I tried to explain how it worked with the meditation and to have patience and give it time, the more I realized that she was not grasping that part at all. She wanted complete peace of mind, and she wanted it now! In the same way that she would probably use an Ibuprofen to quell a headache. And our meditation wasn't delivering the goods.

It's around this time that I realised there was probably a fair sized gap between the stuff we talked about when teaching newcomers how to meditate, and what was becoming an increasingly common problem - people being far too stressed to hang around patiently hoping things would get better. In the past we had become used to people coming to us to start on a spiritual journey of discovery, so it was hard to adjust to those who were looking for something altogether more basic - a headache pill for their thinking, something to shut down the panic, anxiety, pain, and stress of their current situation.

That's when the idea for this book was born, and so I started writing. The interesting thing about this whole exercise is how fascinating it becomes when you tie together the power of true meditation with an understanding of how the mind works with 'reality.' The more I delved deeper into the physiological side of our mind and consciousness, and learned about the interconnection between mind, body and meditation, the more fascinating it became. We are incredibly complex and intricate beings, and yet at the same time, paradoxically, everything boils down to a delicious primordial simplicity. We create our universe. As our mind goes, so goes our life experience.

Sure we can get hit by a truck and spend months in hospital, and it probably wasn't our mind that created the accident, but a significant part of how well we heal and how quickly we can get back on our feet again, will come from our mental approach to the injury and circumstances. In everything we do, our mind is the rudder of the ship and we can either let noxious events drive us into a dark cul-de-sac, or we can navigate through it all with the delicacy of a ballerina en pointe.

*Every night and every morn*
*Some to misery are born,*
*Every morn and every night*
*Some are born to sweet delight.*
  William Blake, Auguries of Innocence, 1863.

Of course it's important not to be flippant about the very real impact of stress on lives, but at the same time I have seen enough real live evidence of how powerfully effective meditation can be in helping to dissolve the problem to know that it works. The one sure constant is the fact that if you devote the time diligently to the meditation, it will – without question – see you through the tough times much better than a quart of vodka or a box of Valium will. And what's more it will deliver moments of absolute joy during the process, which is almost miraculous.

So the key message of this book, for those of you who may be reading to try and learn how to handle a stressful episode or situation is, don't give up. You can transcend the situation you're in, or the event you've just suffered, if you are patient and determined. Just keep to a regular practice of an authentic meditation, and manage the things you can manage. Time and your growing power of detached observation will do the rest. And above all, remember that nothing is ever random.

Because if there's one thing I've learned as I've moved through two decades of life as a meditator, it's the fact that there's an order to the chaos, and a route we're ushered along which gives us the opportunity to make of this life what we can. The choices may not always be opulent, and things may even be brutal at times, but as long as we maintain an open heart and calm determination, we can emerge intact, cherished and humbly triumphant.

The bottom line is this book, along with the companion free email meditation course, should provide a solid foundation on which to base your fight against the perils and pain of stress in many of its most debilitating forms.

# - FORWARD -

There are a large number of self-help books on the shelves which deal with the growing problem of stress in the world, so it was interesting to be asked to provide a forward to this particular one. The work that we as cognitive neuroscientists do in studying the brain patterns of our thoughts and emotions, in particular in mental disorders, is very pertinent to the subject of stress and anxiety, as it is clear that thoughts and emotions are inextricably linked and can trigger stress.

Of course psychologists and psychiatrists also have their expertise to add to the subject, although from a neuroscience point of view we look more at the underlying brain mechanisms, rather than the nuance of thought and emotion. Our job is to understand the brain mechanisms that underlie normal and abnormal thought and emotion processes. However, as every neuroscientist will confirm, this is not a simple matter, especially when it comes to mixing in the emotional and mental conflicts that we often see at the heart of a stressed personality.

I have had the privilege to focus my work on some of the most deprived people in society, abused youngsters from socially dysfunctional homes, and from this have learned a lot about the impact that stressful conditions, you might say chronic conditions, can have on the structure and working of the human brain.

We see all types of stress in our research, and plot the implications of these disorders with our instruments, but it is only when you encounter the reality behind poverty, abuse and neglect that you really get a sense of how much damage chronic stress can have both on a personality and on their brain, especially a young one. As the author suggests early on in this book, stress is a product of our thinking, and at its most extreme our thoughts can literally ruin our health, as well as our happiness.

As a neuroscientist who works in mental illness I can agree with this. High levels of stress are not only pertinent to people with trauma and abuse, mostly leading to post-traumatic stress disorder, but are present in most mental disorders. Living with a mental disorder is stress. I have come to realise in my work that most psychiatric disorders suffer from some form of thought disorder, be it paranoid thinking in schizophrenia, obsessive thoughts in obsessive-compulsive disorder, mind-wandering in Attention Deficit Hyperactivity Disorder or rumination in depression.

These abnormal thought processes are closely linked and likely trigger all the other mental and emotional problems these patients have. Mental illness, however, is just the extreme end of a continuum, and the same applies to the normal population. Our thoughts can trigger stress. The problem is that stress, whether mental or emotional, as Powell argues, is amplified in our busy city-dwelling society by the constant bombardment with visual and auditory noise. This provides an information overload we find difficult to cope with. Studies have in fact shown that information overload leads to depression and dissatisfaction.

Prolonged use of social media sites such as Facebook, for example, has been shown to be associated with increased ill-being and lower self-esteem, and the mediating factor is thought to be the overload of the constant stream of data which our brains are expected to process as we browse these services (Kross et al., 2013). This type of continuous mental strain makes it difficult for us to focus our attention on any one single thing. Because our attention is continually being torn between email, social network messages, YouTube videos and news feeds, we find it ever harder to focus our attention on one single object for any longer than 10 minutes at a time.

As an example of how bad this is getting, modern online education over the Internet is progressively being adapted to match the increasingly short attention span of the modern internet student, which may be making the situation even worse. Imagine a classroom one day where the length of the lessons are kept to less than 10 to 15 minutes!

This information overload not only leads to a scattered mind and attention but also affects our emotions. For example, studies have shown that not just social media but also media multitasking has been associated with depression and anxiety (Becker et al., 2013). Small wonder then that people become desperate for relaxing nature holidays, as Powell points out, where they can feel the benefits of a calm and quiet environment without the constant noise pollution affecting their minds.

The key message of this book is the rejuvenating and healing power of silence, which is obtained through regular meditation. The solution to the problem which Powell offers follows logically from what he suggests is the root cause of stress. If the root cause of stress lies in our noisy mind, we need to reduce our thinking through meditation and combat the mental noise with mental silence.

The goal is to think less, reduce this mental clutter, and ultimately enter a space of mental peace which gives us the experience of the here and now. Even a few minutes a day of mental silence, so Powell argues, will help us to reduce the stress which is caused by all the mental activity and worries we constantly carry with us.

However, meditation does not only help with the mental stress of over-thinking, it also helps with emotional stress. Powell's view is that the mental silence experienced in meditation helps us to become more detached and achieve an emotional distance from the situation, which gives us greater emotional resilience and, in addition, allows us to deal with the problem in a more efficient way.

We all experience negative life events, such as the loss of a parent, a loved one, or a partnership. We know from psychology that it is how we cope with the emotional stress that determines our stress levels and consequently our physical and mental health. Powell suggests that an important side effect of the experience of mental silence in meditation is that we gain a more detached and dispassionate perspective of things, which makes us more resilient to such stressful life events.

Interestingly, more and more scientific research is backing up this claim. Studies have demonstrated that meditation can lead to greater physical, emotional and mental detachment (Aftanas et al., 2005), and it is the frequency of the mental silence achieved through meditation that has been shown to lead to improved general and mental health. This suggests it can therefore be considered as an effective way to prevent and mitigate illness (Manocha et al., 2012).

As you will see in the book, this type of research seems to confirm the theory that meditation has benefits on our physical, as well as mental, health. However stress reduction is probably the single most documented effect of meditation, which has been shown to be due to the activation of the parasympathetic nervous system that relaxes and restores bodily functions.

Brain imaging studies have also shown that meditation leads to a reduction of the type of brain activity that corresponds to mental clutter or mind-wandering, which has been associated with better attention (Sood et al., 2013). The inverse is also true, people with attention deficits seem to suffer from excessive mind-wandering and mental clutter, which they can't switch off when they need to concentrate, and this contributes to their attention difficulties (Rubia et al., 2014). Interestingly, the inability to switch off the mental clutter is being progressively observed in most other mental disorders, not just attention disorders.

These scientific finding are in line with Powell's hypothesis that meditation reduces stress, not just via a direct effect on the parasympathetic nervous system, but also indirectly, through reducing the thought processes that cause us to be stressed. Thus, at the very least, the meditation training will reduce your mental clutter and improve your attention, even if you achieve nothing else, which implies that meditation is in essence also a valuable form of attention training.

Therapeutically, many studies have also shown that meditation works as a treatment for a host of diseases ranging from physical to mental disorders (Rubia, 2009). The therapeutically effective factor appears to be the achievement of the state of mental silence and its frequency, which again supports the ideas that Powell puts forward in this book about the importance of managing our attention with the assistance of regular meditation. The hypothesis of this book, that our thoughts and their close link to our emotions are the root cause of stress, fits in with what we observe and understand as scientists, and is interestingly also in line with the kind of ancient wisdom described by Lao-Tse, Buddha, and many other eastern and western mystics.

So it seems logical to suggest that the solution to stress follows on from the analysis of the problem: stop or reduce your thinking and you will reduce your stress levels. The instructions and meditation exercises given here in this book to reduce our mental noise are relatively simple and easy to follow. The rest is up to you, the user!

Katya Rubia
*Dr Katya Rubia is Professor of Cognitive Neuroscience at the Institute of Psychiatry, King's College London, UK.*

## REFERENCES

Aftanas L, Golosheykin S. (2005) Impact of regular meditation practice on EEG activity at rest and during evoked negative emotions. Int. J Neurosci. 2005 Jun;115(6):893-909.

Becker MW1, Alzahabi R, Hopwood CJ. (2013) Media multitasking is associated with symptoms of depression and social anxiety. Cyberpsychol Behav Soc Netw. 16(2):132-5.

Kross E, Verduyn P, Demiralp E, Park J, Lee DS, Lin N, Shablack H, Jonides J, Ybarra (2013) Facebook use predicts declines in subjective well-being in young adults. O. PLoS One 14;8(8):e698841.

Manocha R, Black D, Wilson L. Evid (2012) Quality of life and functional health status of long-term meditators. Based Complementary and Alternatative Medicine 2012; published ahead of print; doi: 10.1155/2012/350674

Rubia, K. (2009) The neurobiology of meditation. Biological Psychology 82(1):1-11.

Rubia, K., Alegria A., Brinson H (2014) Imaging the ADHD brain: disorder-specificity, medication effects and clinical translation. Expert Review of Neurotherapeutics, in press.

Sood A, Jones DT (2013) On mind wandering, attention, brain networks, and meditation. Explore (NY) 9 (3):136-41.

*[Note: Live links to all the references in this book can be found at www.meditationforstress.net/references which can also be accessed directly on your phone using the QR code on the Resources page at page 151].*

# - CHAPTER 1 -

## Introduction

If you're reading this, chances are there's stress somewhere in your life. Either you or someone you know or love may be facing some sort of stress related issue. The goal of this book is to help sufferers deal with the issue in a practical way, through the use of meditation and simple mental exercises designed to dissolve the trauma at source.

Stress hurts everyone it touches, and when severe enough it can even kill, so proper early attention to the treatment is essential. There are lots of methods available for treating stress but the solution we propose here is different. As we'll see later on, the program outlined in this book relies on an effective form of meditation based around the idea of emptying the mind of thoughts. By dealing with the thoughts which trigger stress, we can defeat the suffering it causes at the source.

## The Unruly Mind

Lurking quietly in the corner of any conversation we can have about stress is a 600lb gorilla, otherwise known as the mind. Our thoughts, emotions and awareness are still quite mysterious, despite the huge strides taken by science and the improvement in our understanding of how the brain works.

The stress we experience takes root from a number of places inside our head, which is why we have a limited number of ways to fight it, without resorting to mind-numbing drugs or other artificial means. This '*unruly mind*' (from the Chinese *xinyuan*) [1] delivers the cascade of thoughts which permeate our mind and trigger the stress we feel. Psychiatrists and psychologists have increasingly focused on helping us understand the mechanics of these stressful thoughts, by showing how our harmful (or maladaptive) thinking can amplify stress, thereby establishing a pattern of mental activity that magnifies negatives and destructively over-generalises situations. In effect we ignore not only the positive aspects of life events, but also reality as well.

These techniques, which include Cognitive Behaviour Therapy, have been shown to help the treatment of stress by encouraging people to take a detached look at their thoughts to see them for what they are, rather than be sucked into the destructive pattern of negativity they can generate. The problem with these approaches is they do not deal with the underlying issues from which these maladaptive thoughts occur, namely the inability of most people to stop the perpetual flow of thoughts, resulting in a constant flood of negative mental activity (or clutter) which eventually dominates the personality.

There have been recent moves to introduce elements of different meditation techniques, such as mindfulness,[2] to the treatment of stress, in order to combat this tendency, but none of them deal with the core issue, which is the fact that many people are simply overwhelmed by a constant torrent of destructive thoughts, which defeat all attempts at positive modification. What is needed is something which can actually help to slow the thought stream, and so dissolve the potential for stress at its source.

What makes the program of treatment outlined in this book so different is the fact that it offers a permanent way of reducing the mental trauma which can cause the symptoms of stress. In effect the program helps the individual to become more immune to stress. Unlike similarly targeted programs such as stress inoculation therapy (SIT), the process here does not involve visualisations, simulations or mental scenarios, but instead relies on the power of the meditation to fundamentally alter the mental patterns in the brain which cause the stress to become so acute in the first place.

This spontaneous and automatic process does not call for any mental gymnastics, because the meditation is its own actor, and the sufferer only has to commit to doing the meditation every day in order for it to produce its powerful and beneficial effects. This process is not a quick fix, as it requires commitment in much the same way an athlete has to commit to a long term program of training and mental development in order to achieve their optimal level of competitive fitness.

The good news is the results from regular meditation can be startling, both in scope and effectiveness. This means it is possible to measure progress right from the beginning, and if all that's wanted is a temporary 'sticking plaster', then that's all that you'll get. However practitioners who wish to use the full toolbox and 'immunise' themselves against future attacks, will need to give it more time to work. The reason this takes time is because the healing process follows a natural rhythm, rather than proceeding at the kind of artificially enhanced speed which we often expect in the modern world.

In the same way a bandage can only temporarily help with a wound, so too this program will at first only provide limited relief of the pain from stressful situations. It can take several months, and probably longer depending on circumstances, for the full long term effect of the meditation to deliver deep seated peace, but once it takes root your life will fundamentally change for the better. In a similar vein, we should not expect to 'understand' the mechanics behind everything we experience in the earliest days, but instead should focus on the experience of the process day to day. We don't need to understand nuclear fission to switch on a lamp, and in the same way we can reap benefits from the program without locking down every detail. Everyone's user manual will be different, so the winners will be those who settle down to enjoy the journey rather than focus on a distant destination, and who push any goals or intellectual demands to the side. The journey will be exhilarating if you can focus on the present moment, because you will experience things you never thought were possible. The key to the program is simplicity, and so those who don't over- complicate their approach will inevitably reap the rewards later on. So is this a guaranteed solution to the huge global problem of stress, you may ask. Well, the answer is a qualified yes. If you follow the program diligently and with an open mind, your life will change for the better. Not because you willed it so, but because the meditation delivers a fundamental change in your world-view in subtle and yet powerful ways, as we will discover later. It's not necessary for you to 'believe' anything to profit from the practice. It will work whether you believe or not, in the same way aspirin cures a headache without you thinking about it. The program delivers what it delivers without a need for any belief, dogma or ritual.

The bottom line is that severe stress can destroy lives, and the problem is becoming more acute, especially in the Western world. It seems that the more 'developed' and complex our societies become, the more negative is the impact on our psyche. The fragile and sensitive members of society typically crumble first, but all levels of society are equally as vulnerable to the problems of our imbalanced lifestyles. Increasing numbers of health professionals are now stating their belief that stress may be the cause of many of our physical and mental problems.[3] Stress appears to play havoc with our delicate physiological and biological systems, and it's now becoming clear just how harmful this can be over the long term.

## GOAL

The goal of this book is to provide a framework within which the meditation can be understood, and within which the practitioner can manage expectations and results. Because the aim is to reduce our mental clutter significantly during the process, the book shouldn't be thought of as merely a user manual, but more like a reference title, which can help make sense of milestones as they occur.

Without a regular practice of meditation this book can offer very little relief for the symptoms of stress, as it is only through the power of mental silence or thoughtless awareness that the real work is done. By all means use the book as a starting point and reference point for the process, but do understand that your meditation is the absolute key to any successful outcomes from the program.

One final point. This program focuses primarily on the treatment of moderate to mild stress and its causes, and while it can help with severe and chronic stress relief, it is always preferable to seek the advice of a qualified health professional, who can provide direct personal treatment specific to a condition. Fortunately there can be many additional side benefits for those who do include this meditation practice in their treatment. These can include key positive changes in attitude, improved mental acuity and even a renewed sense of purpose in life. The results may surprise, and in some cases shock, practitioners, but at the heart of this process of self-awareness there will generally be a new sense of understanding and self-respect. The beauty locked inside each of us doesn't need much prompting to emerge bashfully into the daylight, and this simple yet powerful program can be the catalyst to help that happen in a very real and delightful way.

## REFERENCES
1. http://en.wikipedia.org/wiki/Mind_monkey
2. http://en.wikipedia.org/wiki/Mindfulness
3. http://psycnet.apa.org/psycinfo/2004-15935-004

NOTES

# - CHAPTER 2 -

## OVERVIEW OF STRESS

What is stress?

Let's try and answer that question by first stepping back and asking 'what is pain'? The dictionary defines pain as '*the neural process of processing noxious stimuli*', but beyond that dry explanation we don't have much more to go on. What it boils down to is simple - pain involves chemical reactions to electrical impulses on nerve receptors in the skin and body parts. But exactly how that translates into 'feelings' of pain is really a mystery, even to the scientists.

There are many different mysteries about the working of pain in the body (including the phenomenon known as 'phantom' pain, which strikes a significant proportion of amputees after a limb has been removed) and in the same way there are a large number of questions still hanging over the concept of stress. Because when you get right down to it, stress – and pain – are different buds on the same tree, in that they both involve a mental reaction arising from an event of some sort.

Nowadays the common understanding of biological stress is anything that disrupts a person's natural equilibrium to a greater or lesser degree. To qualify as stress in the context of our well-being we tend to treat it as an ailment in its own right, so we say that someone suffers from 'stress'. This shorthand of course really means 'they are suffering from some situation which is causing them to be stressed - i.e. out of balance'.

The human being is designed to cope with stress, because it is a natural part of existence. When we were cave dwellers we would be stressed by the hunt, or by an encounter with a known predator, with the very need for survival in an incredibly hostile environment. The kind of stress primitive people experienced was a far more real, life or death stress than we experience today.

Nowadays in our civilized world, the type of stress we experience may not involve day to day survival of climate, famine or attack, but the effects can be almost as severe in the long term. Much of the stress we feel today in the Western world is also light years away from the horrors of living in a war zone, or suffering poverty and malnutrition in a developing country, but again, the impact of our 'First World' problems can still be devastating. We suffer from complex layers of stress which come from an environment which places huge demands on our cognitive abilities to an extreme degree.

The fear of losing our jobs, health, taxes, rules, laws, regulations, ethical and moral demands and even relationships, are just some of the things which threaten our equilibrium every single day of the year. What's different nowadays is the fact that there are so many potential sources of such pain, whereas back in primitive times the list of things that would trigger your anxiety was probably smaller (even if many of them were definitely more deadly!)

Modern day stress may no longer be triggered by the proximity of a man-eater or an aggressive neighbouring clan, but the actions of a predatory abusive boss playing office politics can probably degrade our physical and mental health to almost the same state if we have to suffer it for long enough. The problem is not just the quantity of environmental opportunities for us to be stressed, but also the fact that these stresses are compounded by the societies we live in.

It's not hard to see how engrained stress is in our lives today. Just take a look around and you'll see that many of the most successful industries exist specifically to profit from our anxiety.

Insurance, the legal profession, even the advertising and fashion industries make huge sums of money from trading on our fears and uncertainty. We fear death, poverty, ill health, criminals, fraud, contractual breach, weight gain and a thousand other aspects of the modern life, which deliver a constant stream of mental turbulence. And for each of these instances, our bodies react automatically even if we don't consciously recognize it.

Our biological '*fight or flight*' system was originally designed for the extremes of primitive living, and the need to survive the occasional life threatening situation, but it's just as ready to spring into action if we receive an overdue phone bill. It doesn't matter whether it's life threatening or not, or if we even realise that we're stressed or not, the subtle underlying damage that the body's '*emergency reactions*' can trigger can still be as severe over the long term.

Every time our autonomous defensive mechanism is triggered, a little bit of physical equilibrium is lost, as our body delivers extra support for our apparent need to react. More than ten different components of our beautifully delicate metabolic system work together to prepare the right reaction, from the adrenal gland to the various parts of the brain which govern memories, emotions and our metabolic systems.

This reaction is designed to save our lives in the short term, a bit like running a car at really high speed to get out of danger, and evolution has clearly proven that it is highly effective at saving lives. However it occurs with little consideration for any long term consequences. So, just as we can wear out our car very quickly by driving as if it was always an emergency, so too does over-use of these emergency systems wear out our body in the long term.

It's quite obvious when a mental nervous breakdown occurs because of this situation, but more medical professionals are becoming convinced that many of our modern ailments, severe and otherwise, are also in fact a by-product of the constant unconscious war being fought inside our bodies. [1]

As we'll see later, a little stress is also good for us, and in fact even has a name. Eustress is the type of stress which we find invigorating as we enter into a challenge, or complete a difficult but enjoyable assignment. Without this sort of benign stress which stimulates us we would definitely be operating on a sub-par level, so the key as with many things is balance. Not too much stress or too little.

### THE PROFIT AND POLITICS OF FEAR
We live in a modern world which profits from our fears. The beauty industry benefits from our fear of getting old and unloved, the security industry from our fear of attack, the insurance industry from our fear of financial loss and ruin. And so on.

Every single day we are faced with marketing which preys on these subconscious fears in order to sell us something, even the retail industry is not blameless. The next time you're in a supermarket or local store, try counting the number of products which covertly or overtly pander to our real or irrational fears of something or other. Beauty products cater to our fear of ageing and loneliness, anti-bacterial wipes to our worry about germs, fad diet products prey on our anxieties about being fashionable and respected.

The list goes on. Each day billions, if not trillions of dollars are earned solely through preying on our fears and anxieties, and what's worse, this drip feed marketing itself helps to increase the mental anguish, which makes it a win-win for the global conglomerates. The more they advertise the perils, the more concerned we become, the more they sell...which gives them revenue to do more advertising. And so on. What a wonderfully elegant system.

As well as this baseline fear marketing, we are also faced with a constant stream of news from a world which seems to have gone crazy, even when we suspect it's just sensationalism. Judging by the amount of prime time devoted to terrorism on the daily news you'd think we were in imminent danger of being hit by an attack. But in reality we're more likely to die of a lightning strike. [2] The media fosters and profits from our anxieties, so the more disasters they can put on the front page or 9 o'clock news, the more advertising they'll sell, and profit they'll make.

It may sound cynical, but it's a fact that every day we swim in a sea of alarm bells, each of which adds to our inner sense of imbalance and anxiety. Some problems are so acute, such as climate change and shrinking global resources that we subconsciously push them to the back of our attention as much as we can. We just can't cope. In any given year nearly 7 million Americans and 2% of Europeans will suffer from a GAD (general anxiety disorder) and GAD is acknowledged as the most common cause of disability in the workplace in the USA. [3]

These fear based profit centres drip feed a constant level of unease into our minds every day, which in turn raise our stress levels to the point where they become more than just uneasy feelings.[4] And when this is combined with additional demands from our general decision making and other mental activities, we get a perfect storm of mental stress which can overload our system to an unstable extent.

Through meditation we become more immune to the noise which tries to unsettle us, and we begin to see it all for what it really is. We also mentally adjust to a world where uncertainty is not something to be afraid of, and in fact it's often an opportunity for us to explore our inner strengths and abilities. By realizing that our constant hunt for that perfect feeling of stability and security is an impossible dream, and in fact is something which can actually impair our personal growth, we can break out of the imaginary mental prison, and start to live life properly. Uncertainty energizes us, it gives us the chance to see who we really are, deep down, and takes us away from the superficiality of a mundane life of routine. Once we recognize the fictional nature of most of our fears and anxieties, we stop worrying about the future and start to enjoy the present, bolstered by the peace we gain from our meditation every day.

## THOUGHTS AND DESIRES

Of course thinking is a fundamentally natural part of the human condition, without which we would soon perish, however few would argue that our modern lifestyle creates more mental chores than we have ever faced before in history. From the moment we are able to start thinking clearly as young children we are faced with a growing number of decision demands, each with consequences layered upon consequence.

As children we must select toys, foods, friends, activities and other factors from a multitude of choices. We learn to express our desire for this situation or that situation, and are encouraged to express our preferences almost from the moment we can talk, and from there it rapidly goes downhill. By the time we're at college, we're expected to think our way to success, through stressful examinations, career choices, intense personal relationships and more. Small wonder that we talk about teenage angst.

And of course adulthood just heaps more onto the pile. Jobs, marriage, security, health, wealth and more pounding on our system day after day after day. And we wonder why we get tired so quickly? The Buddha stated that desire is the cause of all human suffering, and it's clear that we are now living proof that of the accuracy of his timeless insight. Each of the demands placed on our heads by our modern lifestyle not only requires a requisite expenditure of mental energy, but also a decision! An expression of our desire manifested by a thought. We decide, therefore we are!

Now decisions per se have never hurt anyone (unless we're talking about stupid ideas relating to treacherous rivers and reckless midnight skinny dipping) but the sheer weight of decision making demanded by a modern lifestyle is now at incredible levels. Imagine a steady stream of stress signals coursing through our bodies as we make decisions about the family home, job requirements, children's upbringing and more.

Should we be surprised when we learn that moving home and getting divorced are two of the most stressful situations we can ever face? [5] According to the Holmes and Rahe Stress Scale (see page 42), any number over 300 indicates an individual is at risk of actual physical illness, just from stressful thoughts. So yes, thoughts are the fundamental building block of modern stress. It is not the fact that your mother is going in for a routine check up of a bump on her nose that is stressful, it is the fact that in the week before it happens, your mind runs through every possible combination of possible reasons for the bump that exist. We can literally go through a mental shredder working out all the permutations of possible scenarios. Yet another stressful event to add to the monthly list.

### Types of stress

The American Psychological Association defines three types of stress which commonly occur around the world. They range from short term, event based situations, to very long term chronic stress, which literally can be a killer if left untreated.

* *Eustress*

We all need a small amount of stress in our lives, because this is the type that stimulates our imagination, helps us to push forward on projects and generally progress in life. Without it, we would be not fulfilling our potential as a human being and a member of modern society. This Eustress is generally short term, feels exciting and helps improve our mental and physical performance.

It's the kind of stress we experience if we receive a promotion at work, start a new job or get happily married.

Even leaning a new hobby can be a positive force because it makes us step outside our comfort zone, which adds to our life experience. This type of positive stress is an essential part of our personality, and because it's short term it doesn't harm us in the same way that long term distressing experiences do. This is why we can enjoy the experience rather than fear it, and why many people talk about 'thriving' on the stress of their job, project to project.

* *Acute*

This type of stress is related to events which occur sporadically, and usually in the near past or upcoming future.. These life events typically involve short term issues, such as a car accident, or a theft or burglary, and they cause us emotional distress as we try to deal with them. They can also cause us to suffer physical ailments such as headaches, stomach aches, muscle pain such as a stiff neck and more hidden problems such as elevated blood pressure. On the whole though, this type of stress is not so severe as the other two types, and with some care and attention can be treated relatively easily.

* *Episodic acute stress*

This form of stress is something that affects a certain type of personality, rather than involving particular situations. This stress is typically suffered by those people who seem to live perpetually chaotic and out of control lives. They're constantly running to catch up, and because they're not fully in control, or take on too much so they can't cope, they end up being tense, irritable, maybe even aggressive.

These people wouldn't admit to being stressed, but in real terms they're living with a continual underlying current of pressure which takes its toll. The type also includes those who are permanent worriers, for whom everything can go wrong, because they invariably try to fix things that don't really need fixing and so add to the workload which is already too high to manage. The unfortunate thing about this type of insidious stress is it's seldom given the recognition it deserves, which means it can go untreated until it's almost too late. Sufferers often experience general levels of ill health, including migraines, hypertension, insomnia and in extreme cases heart attacks and disease.

★ *Chronic stress*

Possibly the most serious form of stress to treat is that experienced in the long term, driven not by personality or situations, but by general environmental triggers. Grinding poverty, long term or acute illness, a hated job or an unhappy marriage can all lead to a fundamentally debilitating form of underlying stress in an individual. As can childhood trauma of any kind. Again it's often unrecognised as the sufferers often '*get used to it*', and resign themselves to an existence with no hope of remission, and an interminably fraught future. This type of stress is clearly hard to treat, because it involves significant life changes, which in turn require recognition of the need to change, with all the upheaval that involves.

In cases such as illness or poverty, there may in fact be no real possibility of a direct change, but in these cases meditation can help to bring the situation into some sort of perspective and thereby reduce the impact of the environment on the individual in a positive way. This form of stress, if left unrecognised for a long period, can lead to the desperation of suicide, violence, ulcers, heart attacks and possibly even contribute to illnesses such as breast cancer. [5a]

## WHAT FEEDS OUR STRESS?

This is both an easy and hard question to answer. The short response is to point to anything that causes us anguish in any way, but if we dig even deeper we'll find that there are many different layers of effects which generate the thing we commonly know as 'stress'. The pyramid below outlines some of the more common structures underlying psychological stress, but of course there are many other aspects of the issue which vary from person to person.

Typically there is an event or situation of some sort which acts as the immediate trigger. This can take many forms, ranging from a bereavement or illness all the way to the loss of a mobile phone in a taxi. Because the final result, stress, occurs inside our mind it is subject to all the mental clutter which either enhances or subdues the effect.

We are confronted with a multitude of 'life events' every single day, and some of them will create stress in some people, while the very same events will be ignored by others. There's no real quantifiable pattern to it. What we can say is there's a process which occurs which ignites the stress inherent in a situation, and the process is fairly simple to explain.

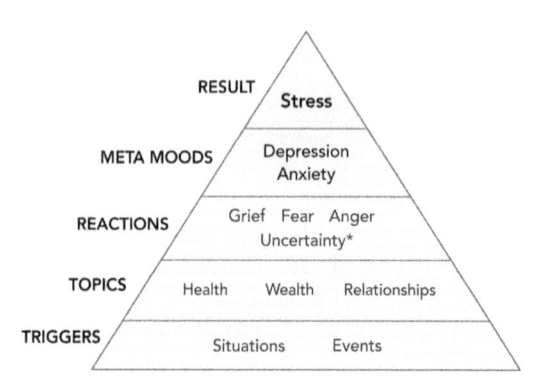

| | |
|---|---|
| RESULT | Stress |
| META MOODS | Depression Anxiety |
| REACTIONS | Grief  Fear  Anger  Uncertainty* |
| TOPICS | Health  Wealth  Relationships |
| TRIGGERS | Situations  Events |

\* other reactions include exhaustion, irritability, nervousness, etc.

Let's say a situation or event occurs...
We react to this situation mentally, probably due to a combination of our emotions and intellect, the environment or

some other factors. However, what starts out as a benign mental process to cope with the situation or event, can quickly become toxic as our thoughts start to expand the issue in our mind. We start 'stressing' to use a popular word, about the situation. And that's where it starts. Now the key thing is the severity of this 'stressing' of course, and we should also remember that there are forms of stress which don't involve conscious thought patterns, but which still seem to do the same kind of subtle damage.

Few people would suggest that they 'stress out' over going out for a meal to a restaurant, but for an unlucky minority the experience may be incredibly stressful for any of a number of reasons. They may have contracted food poisoning in a restaurant, or been accosted on the way home or simply been brought up to mistrust the food or wasteful nature of the dining experience. But for the vast majority of people, dining out is a treat and a definitely pleasurable thing to enjoy. What this means is the reality behind this event occurs not outside, but actually inside each of us – in general our thoughts make a situation good or bad. And these thoughts can come from any cause in our lives.

The Stress Scales from Holmes & Rahe (example shown below) calculates the potential for stressful impacts from a large variety of situations. A score of more than 300 suggests that an

| LIFE EVENT | LIFE CHANGE UNITS |
| --- | --- |
| Death of a spouse | 100 |
| Divorce | 73 |
| Marital separation | 65 |
| Imprisonment | 63 |
| Death of a close family member | 63 |
| Personal injury or illness | 53 |
| Marriage | 50 |
| Dismissal from work | 47 |
| Marital reconciliation | 45 |
| Retirement | 45 |

individual is vulnerable to illness, under 150 indicates they're slightly at risk.

As the 2nd century Stoic sage Epictetus said, "*your will needn't be affected by an incident unless you let it*", which is another way of saying '*it's all in the mind*". And this is where the clue lies in how meditation can help dissolve the stress that we experience. As we'll see later on, the cure comes from using the meditation to mediate between the 'event' and the reaction, so we no longer experience the trauma in any significant way, resulting in low or no stress at all.

It's important to note at this point, that this is NOT the same as suppressing the reaction, as many positive thinking programs recommend. Instead this is a process of dissolving the engine which generates the negative thoughts, which in turn feed the stress in our mind, thereby removing the stress itself. We can think of the engine as the combination of intellect, emotions and conditionings[6] (or reinforced responses) that form our core personality, and the meditation as softly muting our core reaction to events and situations which might otherwise cause upset to occur in our mind.

The other part of the equation involves our growing detachment from desire, which happens naturally over time as we continue to meditate. Generally we desire outcomes, in fact we are again, from birth, trained to cultivate and cherish an attitude of desire for outcomes. We are taught that we have to demonstrate desire in order to gain success, and we're chastised as 'indolent' or 'too stupid' if we don't seek to achieve desirable outcomes in our life. The typical rule nowadays seems to be if you want something, you need to go out and fight for it, to achieve it. Exam success, career success, relationships and so on. In fact we can easily identify the three main components of our acquisitive society as health, wealth and relationships, although not necessarily in that particular order.

These drivers of success...to maintain our youth and vitality, to achieve financial success and establish enviable relationships... underpin most of the misery in the world if you really analyse the facts behind the marketing. However, as the Buddha knew, our desires are never satisfied, because no matter how much we succeed, how much we earn or how amazing our relationships are, there's always something more we want or need.

The mind drives us on in a never ending search for more gratification, and as we'll see later on, this process may even have a chemical root cause which occurs in our brain. The result is that our unending drive for achievement is doomed to dissatisfaction and failure, and while many will say that striving for something is better than simply idly drifting through life, in practice it's a cycle which unfortunately seems to deliver more unhappiness than we should expect.

The result of this constant struggle is the fact that we generate more and more stress for ourselves, as we try to fulfil the impossible dream. How often do we hear even the rich and famous admit to having '*regrets*' in some way or another? No matter how successful people are, isn't it strange how angry or insecure they can seem deep down? The often tragic examples of drugs and alcoholism are a few clues that demonstrate how empty and hollow some of these lives can be.

So we can see that unending material ambition, far from enriching our soul and giving deep satisfaction, actually seems to do the opposite, and yet it is what we have been taught to strive for all of our lives. It's hardly surprising then that we become stressed when we inevitably come up short on these impossible aspirations. Now it would be completely unrealistic to suggest that we should try and remove all desire from our lives, because while this would no doubt suit an ascetic living in a cave on a mountain top, it is clearly highly impractical if you're trying to hold down a steady job in town, pay the mortgage and make sure the children are eating their Ready Flakes every morning. Without that fundamental desire to establish and maintain a stable and secure lifestyle things could start to unwind pretty quickly. But at the same time, it may be time to take stock of our overall approach to life and the acquisition of success and ask whether there's not a more balanced way which might work? If the price of 'success' in whatever form is a life awash in stress, then maybe it's not delivering the optimum experience we could be aiming for, which begs some questions.

The bottom line is we are all subject to an existence which doesn't always go according to the way we think it should go. We make plans and they have to be changed, we desire one outcome and something else occurs, and so on. Whether you believe in a higher power, or think everything is a totally random stream, it's clear that we don't have as much control over our affairs as we would like to think. We can make small adjustments to the steering wheel now and then, but in the main, the important stuff is generally out of our hands completely.

## THE FOUR MYTHS

With this in mind, perhaps we ought to understand that our desire for happiness, achievement, knowledge and freedom - what we can call the Four Myths – are nothing more than illusory elements which in the end leave us vulnerable to a life of dissatisfaction, and in extreme cases mental distress?

Perhaps some examples might help?

Many children in the Western world are taught from an early age to equate happiness with financial security and stable relationships, and so many of us seek these things out as a fundamental part of our life goals. Even where material possessions are not the focus, we learn from early on that we should try to be 'happy', as though that is sufficient for a fulfilling life. And while we may take different routes, and the proportions may differ from person to person, we are still conditioned to look for this ideal concept called happiness. After all even governments and philosophers tell us it is an inalienable right.

But perhaps it isn't? What if life is not designed to be a remorseless hunt for 'happiness', but a gentle meander through a series of life situations which are designed to help us grow as a personality and eventually know our true selves? To delve deep into the hidden but contented core of our soul? Suddenly we can see all sorts of possibilities open up. That failed relationship when we were young? Not a failure at all, but a way to realize that maybe we needed to be a little less selfish in certain matters. The lack of any job satisfaction even as we reach middle age? Maybe a way to ensure that we focus our attention more on a weekend passion, which allows our creativity to flow in full flood? And so on.

As Oliver Burkeman puts it in his book, The Antidote: Happiness for People Who Can't Stand Positive Thinking [7]:

*'[Yet] the ineffectiveness of modern strategies for happiness is really just a small part of the problem. There are good reasons to believe that the whole notion of 'seeking happiness' is flawed to begin with. For one thing, who says happiness is a valid goal in the first place?'*

According to Burkeman, a large proportion of our modern day dissatisfaction comes from constant efforts to achieve happiness by doing away with the terrors of an uncertain future. We don't like uncertainty and so we try to manage it away with as much despatch as we can, but like a pesky cough it just seems to keep coming back to haunt our thoughts.

*'Faced with the anxiety of not knowing what the future holds, we invest ever more fiercely in our preferred vision of that future — not because it will help us achieve it, but because it helps rid us of feelings of uncertainty in the present.'* [ibid]

However, when we turn happiness on its head and recognize it as a possible dead-end route, which can actually obstruct our personal and spiritual growth, we get a whole new perspective on life that can help remove the stressful reaction from our minds in many typical situations. In the same way, we may be able to see achievement and knowledge as by-products of our true road to success, one where we become deeply satisfied souls who do not need accolades in order to feel good about themselves. Nor do we need to '*understand*' everything about our existence and this universe, we can let go of the constant search for '*knowledge*' for the sake of it.

This upending of conventional thinking can even stretch to one of the most emotive words in the language, freedom. We're taught that the struggle for '*freedom*' is one of the most noble causes a person can undertake, and that those who sacrifice everything for this goal are among the greatest personalities of an era. But it's only when we come down to examine the detail of what we mean by freedom, that this concept starts to slip from our grasp.

What is freedom actually? Isaiah Berlin's seminal treatise outlining two possible forms of freedom, positive and negative, demonstrate the problem in defining something which is so open ended.[8] Positive freedom relates to our ability to reach our full potential, while negative freedom, the kind we most often associate with news reports on the television, relates to our freedom from external restraint, as in, for example, freedom from tyrannical or abusive control by others.

So what does this have to do with stress? Well, in simple terms the expectation that we can somehow secure personal freedom, adds to the list of factors which subconsciously drive our sense of frustration with our lives. When you've been told all your life that everyone should enjoy a 'free' existence, and it's clear that you are not, for whatever reason - whether it's because you slave away at a job you hate, or have less money than your peers - then it's easy to become embittered when things don't work out as we are told they should. It's a myth that is hard to shake, and yet true personal freedom is as impossible to achieve as permanent happiness. In order to lead valuable productive lives as members of society we need to forego at least a few personal freedoms in order to fit in and contribute, and that's before we factor in more significant compromises such as abiding by laws and moral structures.

The earliest philosophers and sages and instinctively knew this truth, which is why seekers of true self-realization focused on the spiritual aspect of our being, rather than on physical or material success. As the Tao (or Dao De Jing) says in Chapter 46;

*"There is no crime greater than having too many desires;*
*There is no disaster greater than not being content;*
*There is no misfortune greater than being covetous.*
*Hence in being content, one will always have enough."*

The core part of our stress often arises because we seek to satisfy these insatiable desires, and therefore suffer. Needlessly.

## REFERENCES
1. http://psychcentral.com/lib/stress-a-cause-of-cancer/000754
2. http://www.washingtonsblog.com/2013/09/youre-68-times-more-likely-to-be-hit-and-killed-by-lightning-than-murdered-by-a-terrorist.html
3. http://en.wikipedia.org/wiki/General_anxiety_disorder
4. http://www.healthcentral.com/anxiety/c/1443/143415/watching-increase/
5. http://psycnet.apa.org/psycinfo/2004-15935-004
5a  http://www.webmd.com/breast-cancer/news/20030924/does-stress-cause-breast-cancer
6. http://www.britannica.com/EBchecked/topic/131552/conditioning
7. http://www.amazon.com/The-Antidote-Happiness-Positive-Thinking/dp/0865478015/
8. http://plato.stanford.edu/entries/liberty-positive-negative/

NOTES

# - CHAPTER 3 -

## THE STRESS CREATED BY OUR NOISY ENVIRONMENT

*When one comes to think of it, one cannot help feeling that nearly half of the misery of the world would disappear if we fretting mortals knew the value of silence. Before modern civilization came upon us, at least six to eight hours of silence out of twenty four were vouchsafed to us. Modern civilization has taught us to convert night into day and golden silence into brazen din and noise. What a great thing it would be if we in our busy lives could restore into ourselves each day for at least a couple of hours and prepare our minds to listen to the Voice of the Great Silence. The Divine Radio is always singing if we could only make ourselves ready to listen to it, but it is impossible to listen without silence.* Mahatma Gandhi. 1869 - 1948

We think too much. It's not our fault, our modern lifestyles constantly encourage us to do so. Everywhere we turn there are devices designed to make us worry, react, ponder and decide. These triggers range from advertisements to news, Internet discussions and more, but are probably easier to collectively label as - noise.

The noise level of the modern world is reaching unprecedented levels, you could say unsustainable levels. Where before we could find a corner of the globe without advanced communications, it is now almost impossible unless you are prepared to spend time deep in the heart of an untouched jungle or mountain region. Just try visiting many of the formerly 'remote' parts of the world, and chances are you'll find at least a telephone kiosk, if not access to satellite links and Internet.

Is this a bad thing? Well cultural issues aside, it depends on what effect all this information and communication is having on our lives. In one way we could say the benefits are huge. We have better global education and cultural understanding than ever before. However the reverse side of the coin is the fact that those of us living in the developed world are drowning under a constant barrage of information. Every activity, even leisure time, is now conducted in a frenzy of mental turbulence.

There is no slow time any more. For those in the cities the problem is even more acute, and it's starting to cause problems; with our emotional and physiological well-being, with our relationships and with society at large. People are starting to lose the capacity to operate 'normally', because we literally can't cope. So which comes first, the thinking or the noise? It seems clear that we create all this environmental noise from our thinking, which in turn feeds our mental noise. Descartes summed it up when he said '*cogito ergo sum*' – I think, therefore I am. But what if the actual reality was '*quid cogito ergo sum*'? WHAT I think, therefore I am.

Could it be that we are the creators of our universe via our thoughts? Once we understand how our thoughts might generate the noise of our existence, it's not hard to understand that both noise and silence have a crucial role to play in the quality of our life in general. By using meditation to soothe down our mental noise, we can in turn encourage the reduction in the noise of our environment, even if in small but key ways.

Because the truth is we do not need to run away to the top of a remote mountain to find peace, we can create it ourselves wherever we are through daily introspection. Also, by controlling the level of noise we expose ourselves to every day, we can take more control over our thoughts, and so reduce stress at its source. But let's start at the beginning. With our thoughts and the problems they cause as they interact with our noisy lifestyle.

## THE NOISY WORLD

The world is a noisy place. Not just audible clamour, but the noise from our overloaded visual, spatial and sensory experience. From the second we open our eyes in the morning, to the last fluttering eyelid before sleep, we are subject to a non-stop torrent of noise. Radio, television, advertising billboards, messaging services, email, the Internet, data, information, the telephone, branding logos and messages, verbal conversation. It never stops. We literally swim through a hyperactive mental soup every moment of our waking day.

Take, for example, a simple trip down to our local supermarket to shop. We either take public transport, walk or drive but in each case we have to navigate an environment that is screaming at us every step of the way. In the car we are faced with dashboard controls which demand attention, such as speed, direction and engine indicators, and we drive through a landscape which also demands constant focus. Billboards ask us questions, road signs make us obey, colour coded signs give us signals which need responses.

Even simple things like the ubiquitous traffic light system is designed to shock our system into alertness. The colours red and yellow are deliberately chosen to stimulate our senses and ensure that we obey the signals as we should. Multiply the effect of all of these encounters throughout the course of a single journey and each drive becomes a mental battleground. Even though we learn how to push it all into the background of our mental process, it's still active back there, adding to the overall mental clutter in our mind.

Once we reach the supermarket, we're faced with another level of noise altogether. It's as though we enter a room full of thousands of small children, each one of which is shouting to get our attention. Buy me, special offer over here, really new and improved, 2 for 1 etc. It goes on. Every time our eye meets a word, logo or signage, our brain responds, if only to retrieve a memory of our past experience with that product. By the time we finish the shop we may have experienced tens of thousands of mental encounters with the noise in the store, each one requiring a reciprocal set of conscious or unconscious mental responses from our brain.

### Try this test

If you think this is all far fetched, try this simple experiment. The next time you're walking down a high street or in a mall, try to stop thinking while looking at shop names, window signs and other display items. If you consciously watch your mind, you'll notice that at the very least you are saying the name out loud in your head while reading the store name or sign. And that's just the surface reaction, underneath that initial mental jolt, there's a lot of other memory bank associations kicking into play as you put the thought into perspective.

It's no surprise then that we often take our vacations in the middle of natural surroundings, with beaches, forests and mountains as cures. Mother Nature does not shout at us. On the contrary, she whispers to us in muted, soothing tones, thereby helping our minds to heal and refresh. And what is the effect of all this noise on our mind? How does this environmental and psychological pollution affect us deep in our being? Surely with all the grey matter we possess we should be able to cope with 100 times the inputs, so what's going wrong?

### The Damage Caused By Noise

Doctors now know that there are many different physical effects which arise from loud audible noise. Hearing loss is obvious, but suspected effects include hypertension, sleeping problems, heart rate issues and even problems with mental well-being.[1] But what about visual noise? Man-made artefacts such as billboard advertising and bright illuminated signage, with their loud colours and jarring images are designed specifically to hijack our attention, and in extreme cases this phenomenon has been likened to visual pollution.[2]

In Sao Paulo in Brazil, matters with visual pollution got so bad that the city had to ban billboard and outdoor advertising several years ago, to try and restore some sense of order out of chaos. [3] An act which was followed by Alaska, Hawaii and Bergen in Norway.[3b] Environmental blight such as rubbish strewn streets and uncontrolled landfill also have directly adverse health consequences for anyone living or working nearby[4], and the light pollution from 24 hour advertising and store front signage can disrupt our circadian rhythm and cause problems with sleep patterns. [5]

The above studies highlight some of the more obvious issues, but there are many more effects which can occur from prolonged exposure to the noise pollution from our urban lifestyles. Unfortunately very little research has been done looking into the overall results of living in these noisy, hectic cityscapes, although there are some studies which suggest that the effects on our mental processes alone can be significant.

For example, a study done by Marc Berman and his team from the University of Michigan back in 2009, discovered that college students given a test after both a short walk in a city environment and a nature walk, experienced improved '*directed-attention abilities*' from the nature walk. In other words their attention suffered more distraction after the city walk.

The researchers believe that the impact on the senses that comes from living and working in a city is enough to literally overload our brain, whereas a short time spent in a natural setting restores our thinking processes. Dr Berman points to many city centre parks as an example of town planners recognizing this problem directly, or at least subconsciously. [6]

## FROGS IN A HOT SAUCEPAN?

Other more recent studies[7] demonstrate that urban living with its social stress, noise and light pollution can produce extra activity in the area of the brain associated with stress and anxiety, as though the brain was on heightened alert because of the inherently hostile and unnatural environment. This happens even if the person does not 'feel' particularly stressed at the time, which is even more worrying. Who's to say whether many of us living and working in cities are just like the mythical frog in a boiling pan of water, suffering impaired levels of mental health while thinking everything is fine?[8]

It seems as though we may collectively be descending into a world where the sheer amount of mental traffic assaulting our minds every day could be at the root of many of our modern ailments, and even possibly more severe illnesses. And there are other more subtle effects which may not seem serious, but which collectively can add up to a gradual degradation in the quality of life of our society in general. Let's take a look at a few examples.

a) Sleep Destruction. According to recent statistics, up to 70 million people suffer from insomnia in the USA alone, with 62% reporting that they experience a sleep problem a few nights each week[9]. In the UK, a survey done in 2011 reported that a massive 75% of women and over 50% of men struggle to get to sleep at night, and suffer mental and physical problems as a consequence. They're starting to call it an epidemic, but why are we surprised?

Not only are we expected to ingest ever increasing amounts of data every day, but our increasing use of technology, such as laptops, smartphones and tablet computers is enabling us to process more information for longer periods of the day at a time. And even when we try and enjoy some down-time, we usually end up exercising our cerebral cortex in front of a square boxy device which beams information and entertainment at us to excite our interest. We are simply not giving our brain enough time to recuperate in any 24 hour stretch.[10]

b) Inattention. We now have a distinct medical term for it, Attention Deficit Hyperactivity Disorder or ADHD, but we do not really understand why it happens or what its long term effect can be. This despite the fact that globally over 5% of individuals under 18 are thought to be suffering from the disorder in one way or another.[10a] We also primarily focus on the problem with children, which ignores the fact that a fragmentation of our attention can continue as we grow older, with more serious results.

More and more studies point to an erosion of focus in adults, an inability to maintain concentration for any more than a few moments at a time. We blame the Internet for this decline in attention span - TL:DR, (too long, didn't read) is a phrase which pops up more and more on online discussion boards - but this problem stretches out into just about every part of our society.

For example we simply don't seem to have the time to spend on the type of long form reading we did in the past, because there's too much other information competing for our attention. Information overload is a cliché nowadays, but it spells out the problem clearly if you know what you're looking for. We're happy reading short Facebook posts, but anything more challenging is too much effort.[11]

A typical day consists of wading through an avalanche of email and text messages, a barrage of mobile phone calls which flow into every space in our life, and the demands of coping with more complex and demanding decision making at work and at home. It's relentless and it's constant. Small wonder that our attention is being pulled one way and another, until we literally don't know how to cope.

c) Confusion & Fear. There are other problems that come with an overload of informational noise ...including a mental state which continually triggers our fight or flight response. We may not admit it, but for many people living a busy urban lifestyle, day to day living is a continual battle against our internal fears and confusion. Sound dramatic? Let's take a typical example.

Two of the primary causes of stress for modern man (or woman) are health and financial security, both of which are kept constantly in our attention by a stream of media messages and marketing. We are advised to try this diet or that diet, and not a day goes by without another research lab telling us that one or other part of our lifestyle is likely to make us ill or kill us. We live in fear of doing badly at work, losing our job, home, family, physical wellness, the list goes on. We seem to be permanently at war with a hostile environment which is out to get us. There's no harmony or peace involved in life, and even when we take those long deserved vacations, the experience can leave us more exhausted than before.

Technology also plays its part to disrupt our chance at a peaceful life. We are expected to keep pace with new ways of doing things and the new technologies that are forced on us, and we are routinely faced with adapting to complex new tasks which are based around technological expediency rather than intuitive human interaction. This type of stress even has a name – technostress.[12] If you've ever suffered from trying to get to a human operator on a corporate voice-mail system you'll have experienced another example of the problem.[13]

d) Destruction of Trust. One of the most insidious and damaging result of the increased levels of noise in our lives is the inevitable erosion of trust that comes from access to too much information. The growth of the Internet means we now routinely find ourselves awash in a sea of contradictory advice and supposed wisdom. Everyone can become an online guru, every discussion board and chat room is home to a cadre of 'experts', even if they clearly don't know what they're talking about. Even the most elevated sources of information such as Wikipedia or other professional websites offer advice that can be fundamentally contradictory, confusing and even flat out incorrect. [14]

Just take a look at some of the wildly disparate medical advice that is typically available online and it's clear that there's a problem. So who are we to trust? It only takes a few bad experiences before we start to lose faith in the sea of knowledge, and in effect we train ourselves to become cynical, to be suspicious of every word. The problem is, our civilisation is built on trust. When that fragile but crucial element starts to fail, the result is usually war, bigotry, antagonism and everything destructive that tears our society apart. Without trust we become no better than the lowest form of animal. The antidote to mistrust is a sense of shared purpose and general humanity, which were historically established via local communities. But as our society becomes more remote and technologically sophisticated we're losing that connection.

Our urban lifestyles, with the increased demands and social pressures, are combining with the data overload to make us less trusting and more fearful of the kindness of strangers. It's no accident that the massive social networks on the Internet are focused on delivering more '*friends*' to our lives. It's a tacit admission that real relationships are one of the major casualties of the modern way. And yet these 21$^{st}$ century friends are frequently described by experts as facsimiles of what real-world friends should be. [15]

e) Dulling of the senses. The louder the noise we experience as part of our life, the more our sense organs react, as if to protect us from the problems. In bright light our pupils contract to protect our eyes, in continually loud environments our ears slowly produce extra wax to protect our sensitive drums from damage.

So why are we surprised when our mind does the same kind of thing when faced with information overload on many levels?

Unfortunately, the more our senses dull down, the more the marketeers have to try harder to break through and grab our attention. It's a vicious circle. It is no longer enough for them to give us the facts and let us choose, they now have to shout their message to get us to notice. NEW, IMPROVED, POWERFUL, MASSIVE DISCOUNTS, SENSATIONAL and more. And the result? We tune out even more. Ad blindness is the term that's used on the Internet, but it happens everywhere.

In the same way, the mass media machine can no longer rely on just giving us the bare information, they have to resort to radically increasing the noise they make to attract our attention and sell us their products. We are therefore subject to a constant barrage of outrage marketing, where groups, individuals, nations and constituencies of every size are portrayed as '*incensed*' or '*furious*' as a result of some insult, victimisation or other real or perceived situation. Just take a look at your local news-stand sometime and see how many front page stories feature angry protagonists. Every day the metaphorical pitchforks and torches are deployed in order to sell us more newsprint, television time or magazine features.

Of course we can predict with sad confidence what the result of all this noise is. Our senses start to become dulled to the messages. We become compassion weary and empathetically numb as all the demands start to blur into one long screech of anger, pain or need. The same problem is happening with our culture and entertainment. Desperate producers, directors and impresarios are being driven to extreme behaviour to grab our attention. Art and music has to be more extreme in content, delivery or shock factor, in order to generate sales. Marketing has to be bolder, more pervasive and above all BIGGER in every sense of the word.

It's no longer enough for the movie industry to produce good entertainment, it has to be a '*tent-pole*' blockbuster. Music has to be a smash hit, theatre has to be ground-breaking, thrills have to be breathtaking. This constant struggle to grab our fractured attention is increasingly reaching Olympian heights, in terms of the demands on our senses and its inevitably fading effectiveness. In the meantime, we are beginning to weary of it all, which makes the task even harder. We weary because we're tired. We're battered, stressed, over-loaded and increasingly desperate for a little less noise in our lives. We subconsciously yearn for some peace and quiet.

For many people the only release from this constant state of anxiety is either to retreat to a world inhabited by regular drug or alcohol intake, or to give up altogether and return to a simpler life in a remote setting. However this is a luxury few can afford with the current global economic climate driving most of the jobs into the cities. The percentage of people who regularly use sleeping pills, painkillers, tranquillizers or antidepressants has soared over the past few decades, to the extent that it's estimated that over 75 billion dollars is spent every year in the US alone on this type of medication.[16]

These are incredible numbers and the effects it must be having on our society in general must be significant. It's no wonder that the Western world seems to be gripped by a permanent state of imbalance. And this statistic doesn't include the use of so called '*recreational drugs*' or the hugely debilitating effect of binge drinking and the rising alcoholism problem in many nations, much of it related to stress and associated dysfunction of one kind or another. In the UK alone it is estimated that alcohol is the cause of over 1 million hospital visits each and every year.[17]

Now that's not to say there isn't a legitimate need for some of these pill prescriptions. There are many people who are on antidepressants because they truly need the biological support they provide, but there are also those at the milder end of the spectrum who have been prescribed antidepressants by well intentioned doctors who are unlikely to benefit at all from these drugs.

This is because the scientific evidence is now emerging to demonstrate that while effective in severe depression, antidepressants in general are no better than placebo for mild depression[18]. So why are so many people with milder forms of depression taking them? Most likely it's the result of pharmaceutical companies overreaching the evidence, motivated mostly by commercial concerns. For example Eli Lilly in the US has recently been in the news for pushing a new disorder in children called SCT (sluggish cognitive tempo) through sponsored research, while promoting its ADHD drugs as a treatment. [19] It's situations like this which highlight how easy it is for commercially driven agendas to profit from our fears and uncertainty to sell us their products. Whether we need them or not.

So with the above in mind, it's clear that something drastic needs to be done if our society is to continue to exist in any kind of equilibrium, and whatever it is needs to be put into place now rather than wait for matters to get even worse. Drugs are not a long term solution, psychiatric counselling seems to provide patchy results and is generally too expensive for the majority of the population (and there are not enough psychologists and counsellors available anyway), and asking people to voluntarily relinquish their livelihood to live a simpler life is just unrealistic. So what's the answer?

## SILENCE AS THE CURE
While we may not be able to bring about major short term changes in the psychologically polluted environment within which we live, and the noise that comes from that immersion,

there is one thing we can control - the way in which our mind processes that pollution and the noise that we encounter day to day. The remedial steps outlined in this book use meditation to generate a special kind of inner silence, one which touches on all aspects of our physical and emotional well-being. This cure, which is as old as time itself, will lend itself to any situation and any type of personality. All you need is the will to keep going and the patience to wait for nature to take its course and the healing to occur.

The secret is to harness the power of silence to rebuild the natural order in our personal environment. This is not about sealing ourselves away in a dark room, but using deeply spiritual energies inside ourselves to build a zone of peace within which we can operate, even in conditions of turmoil and uncertainty. The key to the whole process, as we shall see, is to meditate every single day, and crucially to allow the meditation to happen spontaneously, rather than try and DO it in a forced way.

The form of meditation that follows below is aimed at slowing down our thoughts, entering into a state of mental silence where we are totally aware of our surroundings, can hear sounds and bustle around us, but inside our mind we are still and at peace. This '*thoughtless awareness*' as it's called, is the shady grove within which our stress fades away and our balance is restored. We use silence as our cure, and it works! It might take a little while to achieve the experience in the beginning, but once you do manage to achieve this silence in meditation on a regular basis (i.e. preferably every day) then the results will start to show themselves within a few short weeks. Nor is it necessary to turn your back on modern day life and become a hermit. The idea of this meditation is for it to be fully effective even as part of a hectic urban lifestyle.

The program is designed to be as easy to follow and use as possible. There is nothing complicated to remember, no special methods or complex techniques. The idea is to relax and allow ourselves to transition into a state of silent meditation, which will heal, rejuvenate and energize us in a remarkable way. There are no quick solutions to restoring balance to our lives, and it would be misleading to suggest there are. Nature operates at a methodical pace in terms of growth, repair and decay, and we have seen ample evidence over time that this natural pace of existence is the perfect way to conduct a living experiment on yourself, through the use of meditation and mental silence.

As the Mahatma says in the quote above - "*...half of the misery of the world would disappear if we fretting mortals knew the value of silence*"

## REFERENCES

1. http://www.ccohs.ca/oshanswers/phys_agents/non_auditory.html
2. http://en.wikipedia.org/wiki/Visual_pollution
3. http://www.newdream.org/resources/sao-paolo-ad-ban
3b. http://www.amusingplanet.com/2013/07/sao-paulo-city-with-no-outdoor.html
4. http://hku-env-health.blogspot.co.uk/2012/11/visual-pollution-in-hong-kong-by-r-kan.html
5. http://www.ncbi.nlm.nih.gov/pmc/articles/PMC2627884/
6. http://www.findingdulcinea.com/news/science/2009/jan/Are-Cities-Bad-for-You-.html
6b. http://pss.sagepub.com/content/19/12/1207.abstract
7. http://blogs.scientificamerican.com/scicurious-brain/2011/08/16/city-living-and-your-mental-health-is-city-living-driving-you-crazy/
8. http://www.psychologytoday.com/blog/mind-wandering/201208/stress-and-the-city
9. http://www.statisticbrain.com/sleeping-disorder-statistics/
10. http://www.guardian.co.uk/uk/2011/nov/13/insomnia-health-warning-sleep-survey
10a. http://ajp.psychiatryonline.org/article.aspx?articleID=98517
11. http://www.huffingtonpost.com/2010/06/23/reading-isnt-in-decline-b_n_622462.html
12. http://etec.ctlt.ubc.ca/510wiki/Technology-related_Anxiety
13. http://socialanxietydisorder.about.com/od/copingwithsad/a/copephonephobia.htm
14. http://www.telegraph.co.uk/technology/wikipedia/9211336/Six-out-of-10-Wikipedia-business-entries-contain-factual-errors.html

15. http://blogs.hbr.org/2011/12/facebook-is-making-us-miserabl/
16. http://www.addictionbyprescription.com/video.php
17. http://www.nhs.uk/news/2011/05May/Pages/nhs-stats-on-alcohol-hospital-visits.aspx
18. http://jama.jamanetwork.com/article.aspx?articleid=185157
19. http://www.nytimes.com/2014/04/12/health/idea-of-new-attention-disorder-spurs-research-and-debate.html?_r=0

See also
http://phys.org/news/2010-10-flight-path-heart.html
http://www.ncbi.nlm.nih.gov/pmc/articles/PMC1253729/
http://www.anxietyuk.org.uk/2012/07/for-some-with-anxiety-technology-can-increase-anxiety/

## NOTES

# - CHAPTER 4 -

## MEDITATION, THOUGHTS AND THE MIND

*'The mind is a factory of illusions. It creates an inner reality, as opposed to the outer reality of the world. We see colors and shapes, smell odors and perfumes, hear voices and sounds...But the universe is made of particles and waves. The mind translates the world into sensations....None of this is real.'* The Nature of Consciousness. Pierro Scaruffi. 2006[1]

One of the main goals of this book is to help us completely detach ourselves from the triggers which cause stress in the first place. In order to do that, we need to understand how and what these triggers are and how they are formed as thoughts in our mind. By understanding a little more about the nature of how our perceptions, emotions, thoughts and memory work together, we will realise just how easy it is to become enmeshed in thoughts that typically aren't as catastrophic as they seem in the first place.

We all know the brain as the seat of our thinking, but few of us realize just how complex the mechanism is. Not even the scientific community really understands all of the intricate workings of this magnificent organ, and it's fair to say that research work on consciousness itself is still at a very early stage. But despite all of this, we do know some things which are interesting and related to our understanding of stress and the modern world.

Thanks to the wonders of the sophisticated scanning equipment that we now use, we know a great deal about how this mental engine is physically structured, and how it processes the various signals inherent in our thinking processes. The brain is thought to contain over 85 billion cells, and over 100 trillion synapses, which are the key cell to cell communication junctions through which all thought signals pass. The brain works by transmitting electrochemical signals from cell to cell, which then control various functions in the body. These functions include everything from the control of glands which secrete hormones to the movement of muscle groups. All of this work takes a lot of energy, and in a human being up to 25% of our total energy from food goes towards maintaining brain function. It's a very greedy organ.

However, despite the significant advances that have been made by neuroscientists in mapping the various function areas of the brain, we are still unable to explain how the conscious mind is derived from the complex electrochemical activities that are happening all the time inside our head. How we use imagination, why we sleep and what in fact consciousness actually is, are still deeply mysterious questions we cannot answer.

*(scan QR barcode above with your phone to view video)*

But in terms of our basic thinking processes and their impact on stress, we do know that much of our reaction to external events is controlled through the release of the brain's specific chemicals. So for instance, we know that we feel good when dopamine is released into the 'reward circuit' of the brain, the emotional bond between a mother and a child is related to the action of oxytocin on the brain's emotional centres, and we feel anxious or excitable when adrenaline is released into the bloodstream on the orders of the brain.

From this basic understanding, and other research, we can track the impact of external stimuli and events on the flows of chemicals in our body and learn what the effects are. It is from this work that we have built up a picture of the fact that meditation influences the production of 'happy' chemicals such as serotonin and that unpleasant situations often trigger the production of chemicals like adrenaline which are used in 'fight or flight' scenarios when the body prepares itself for an unknown scenario. Of course the stress we feel in uncertain or negative events also triggers these 'fight or flight' chemicals, and it is the prolonged excretion of these intense chemicals that can cumulatively begin to adversely impact our physical and mental states. However when we engage in more gentle pursuits, or enjoy something like art, meditation or music, we do not trigger a fight or flight response, from the body, and instead enjoy the flow of more pleasurable chemicals which deliver relaxation.

### DETACHMENT, MEDITATION AND A BUSY MIND

Of course it's all well and good to talk about chemical triggers and suchlike, but at the end of the day something traumatic like the death of a parent cannot be reduced to some arcane concept of biology. The stress and anguish we feel in traumatic situations is vividly real in our minds, and rightly so. We would be inhuman not to grieve or pine for a loss or a tragedy. However there is also every reason for us to try and minimise the pain of such an event, if only to help us cope with it, and so be able to help others who have also been affected.

The real goal of this stress relief program is to help reduce the initial trauma of stressful life events, and help the mental healing process occur significantly faster, through the use of many different soothing avenues. As we will see, regular meditation really does reduce the mental anguish, but it also reformulates our thinking patterns in general, which in turn helps us develop a mental attitude which is more immune to imbalance.

For example, one of the main ways we can help to overcome anguish or anxiety over something is to fall back on to a sense of detachment about the situation. By detachment we do not mean callous indifference, but more a sense of perspective which acknowledges the situation as it is, and then understands its place in the overall picture. The loss of a parent or spouse is clearly a hugely stressful event, however we know that time heals, and eventually over a period of time we learn to adjust to the loss as best as we can and carry on. With the use of meditation we don't have to 'learn' to adjust, but instead we can use our improved attention to clearly understand the reality behind the process of life and death, and accept it more readily as a natural part of existence, without the level of trauma that is typically associated with the loss of the a loved one.

The cognitive scientists who have developed programs such as CBT (cognitive behaviour therapy) provide specific models for patients to follow to acknowledge the situation and thoughts surrounding this kind of stressful situation, and thereby break the destructive mental and emotional chain which leads to stress. The power of the silence which flows through thoughtless awareness meditation, on the other hand, takes us beyond our mental clutter completely. The meditation lifts us above our thoughts, and instead takes our attention to the reality and beauty of life as it is, helping us to understand that both positive and negative experiences are a valid part of the whole tapestry of living. We don't latch on to the negative aspects of a life event, any more than we let irritating sand in our shoes ruin a day out on the beach.

The detachment that automatically comes from regular meditation also helps us to be more effective with stressful events that need action rather than self-pity, because we avoid being drawn into emotional turbulence which tries to repeatedly re-play the situation in our minds over and over. Woulda, coulda, shoulda is a common pattern of stress filled thoughts, and yet it serves no purpose whatsoever, except in prolonging our panic, pain or remorse. It is this kind of impotent mental activity that is at the heart of most serious stressful experiences; replaying events, experiences, solutions and options over and over again, as if something magical will suddenly happen and everything will be all right again. In reality these thoughts waste valuable time when we could be taking remedial action, time which could be spent more profitably in enjoying what benefits we do still possess from our life and circumstances.

Even the most frail, poverty stricken existence can produce moments of laughter or delight, but it takes the right frame of mind to recognise those opportunities and profit from them. Even those standing at the doorway to death could enjoy their last moments if we knew how to let go of the things that stand in the way. For example, imagine a world where death was not treated as some dreadful, permanent blackness to which everyone was doomed. Imagine instead that death was understood to be a doorway to the ultimate peace, joy and serenity, and we knew this for an absolute fact.

It may sound fanciful, but if it was the case, we would perhaps treat our inevitable progress towards that door in a significantly different way. Without a fear of death a lot of triggers for anxiety drop away, and we're left with more opportunity to enjoy the here and now, instead of worrying about the future. See the Denial of Death[2] for an example of a different way of thinking on this subject.

### Plasticity and bias

Meditation is not a magical wand which can deliver this kind of serene attitude at a stroke, but over time if practised diligently, it does offer a real and powerful sense of purpose and peace which delivers the same kind of result. Most importantly, it breaks a potentially vicious cycle of negative thinking which can arise through chronic stress, where the individual's circumstances are so traumatic that there seems to be no escape. Scientists know that we are all subject to a range of what are known as 'cognitive biases', which reflect systematic mistakes (irrationality?) in thinking that we make all the time.[3] One of the most unhealthy of these is 'negative bias', which makes us remember and over elaborate negative events far more than positive events.

This means that we often find ourselves ignoring the good in a situation, and instead focus on the bad, which over time can become a pattern of behaviour we slip into far too easily for our own good. The sad part is these thoughts are often anything but logical, but we just can't help ourselves.

The good news is that even though we can easily fall into these thinking traps, there is a way out. We know from recent research that the brain has a remarkable capacity to rewire itself in response to our environment and experiences. This *'neuroplasticity'* as the scientists call it, is a relatively new concept, and it overturned our old ideas that the brain was a fixed entity which simply degraded in cognitive quality as we got older.

Now we know that our brain can readily change structure and connections according to situations. So for instance studies have shown that taxi drivers in London have a larger hippocampus region in the brain than London bus drivers. This is not because they're more intelligent (although we suspect there are some cabbies who would disagree) but because taxi drivers need a larger memory area to handle the geographic map knowledge of London, whereas bus drivers simply drive a route every day.[4] In terms of meditation and stress therefore, we would expect to see similar changes in the structure of the brain after long term practice of meditation, and indeed studies suggest that those who have been practising meditation for a long time don't have the same age-related thinning of the inferior frontal lobe of the brain, which is one of the key attention areas.[5]

With this in mind it seems logical to suppose that meditation can have a significant impact on the kind of thought patterns that lead to chronic stress, by breaking the established structures of the brain, to allow for more balanced and positive mental activity to break through. And crucially this change can provide long term benefits for the individual for as long as they continue to meditate. We may, in effect, be able to significantly alter the brain structures which deliver these negative thoughts through regular use of daily meditation. We do know that meditation seems to enhance the resilience to negative life events which are often the cause of chronic and acute stress.[6]

## Moods, emotions and stress

We also know that our moods and emotions are intrinsically tied to our experiences of stress. Stressful events can often trigger emotional responses (e.g. the fear we feel after a close shave with danger) and also longer lived moods, such as becoming severely despondent after losing a job or a loved one.

Emotions are often triggered by events and last for a shorter time than moods, which can often quietly 'creep up' on us, seemingly for no identifiable reason. In their most severe form, these moods can become illnesses, defined as mood disorders, every bit as debilitating as physical ailments. The most common form of mood disorder is probably depression, which also seems to be reaching epidemic levels across the world at the moment. The World Health Organisation reports that depression is currently the leading cause of disability worldwide, and globally more than 350 million people are classified as sufferers from the disorder.[7]

These figures are directly tied in with the growing levels of stress we experience every day, as there is a clear connection between the levels of chronic stress and the risk of developing depression. Once again however, we do know that meditation can effect significant improvements if used in the treatment of depression, both by directly improving the secretion of beneficial chemicals in the brain, and by slowing the flow of thoughts during the meditation, which in turn appears to allow for the general mental state of the individual to improve over time.

## REFERENCES

1. http://www.amazon.com/The-Nature-Consciousness-Piero-Scaruffi/dp/0976553112
2. http://en.wikipedia.org/wiki/The_Denial_of_Death
3. http://www.bbc.co.uk/news/science-environment-26258662
4. http://sharpbrains.com/resources/1-brain-fitness-fundamentals/neuroplasticity-the-potential-for-lifelong-brain-development/
5. http://www.ncbi.nlm.nih.gov/pubmed/17655980
6. http://prezi.com/tqevvoey3hgv/sahaja-yoga-meditation-english/
7. http://www.who.int/mediacentre/factsheets/fs369/en/

NOTES

NOTES

## - CHAPTER 5 -

### MEDITATION, THOUGHTS AND THE PHYSICAL BODY

We use our brain to think, and the brain is nothing more than an organ in the body. As such it is subject to all the same issues that make human flesh vulnerable. If we could somehow insert a special microscope permanently into the body to take a look at the metabolic events that occur during periods of stress in our lives, we'd probably be stunned by the thousands of tiny but crucial chemical changes, processes and triggers which give rise to our thoughts and anxiety and envelop the whole process.

### CHRONIC STRESS AND THE BRAIN

One of the areas which scientists have been investigating over the years is whether the constant load our brain is placed under when we experience chronic, long term stress, is actually physically hurting our brain in some way. The idea that the organ responsible for our thinking could be harmed by distressed thoughts triggered and amplified by stressful situations, is something that could explain why this cycle can become such a destructive force.

It's rather like suffering a feedback loop, where the mind reacts to the stress, which in turn over time creates a brain which is more susceptible to these thoughts in terms of our memory and conditionings. This '*allostatic load*' as it's called, refers to the wear and tear on the body which occurs from long term chronic stress[1]. The term was originally coined by Professor Bruce McEwen from The Rockefeller University, who has studied the long term effects on the brain of hormones which are secreted as a result of chronic stress, particularly in the part of the brain relating to memory and mood. His findings suggest that *'chronic stress reduces neuron number and contributes to cognitive impairment'* which basically suggests that stress induces the same kind of mental degeneration as you might see in someone suffering from Alzheimer's disease.[2]

It seems that what might occur is the stress triggers the release of glucocorticoids, which help fight the stress in the early stages, but actually become harmful to our thinking processes if the stress continues on too long.[3] The research is on-going, but it gives a clue as to the kind of effects stress may have on our physical body as well on our emotional fortitude as the process continues over time. Because these hormones have an effect on remodelling our brain, we can become locked into patterns of thought which are harmful, which makes the problem even more acute. We all know people who seem to be perpetually 'negative', and this physiological aspect may explain why that happens, and why they have such difficulty breaking away from those destructive patterns of thought.

Once again, we're presented with the fact that our thoughts can lock us into a spiralling degradation of behaviour which is harmful to us in more ways than we can imagine. Our immune system becomes impaired, our emotional resilience is degraded and we become much more vulnerable to physical and psychological ailments as time goes on.

## FOOD FOR THOUGHT

Our thoughts are fuelled through the ingestion of energy parcels – otherwise known as food – and our metabolic system converts this food into the glucose energy source that our brain uses day to day. But there is more to this basic statement than just a simple metabolic system at work. The biological processes that make up our body's metabolism are incredibly complex, and this includes the way we convert fuel into power for our muscles, brain and other needs. For example, we have two possible sources of energy available for our needs, glucose which is the typical body 'fuel' and ketones, which is produced by the liver from fatty acids in the absence of glucose (e.g. in the fasting state, while asleep or in nutritional ketosis). The body therefore makes use of a wide range of dietary and stored fuel such as fats and protein to create the energy we need for movement, thinking and general living. It is the ability of the body to react to different states (such as periods of low food availability) with such flexibility that is interesting in terms of how our dietary intake can link to our patterns of thought.

The above is significant because it shows that *'we are what we eat'* really does hold true in many cases that we still don't fully understand. If we remember that our brain uses a good quarter of the body's daily energy requirement, we can see that the demands caused by our thinking can have a profound effect on our overall metabolic processes and vice versa. It is not hard to see that what we eat can directly affect the shape of our thoughts and emotions, and conversely our mental activity can impact the state of our physical body too, literally through over exerting important organs such as the liver.

For example there is some evidence that nutrition plays a direct part in our overall mood and cognitive effectiveness. A 2006 study by Wilkins et al found that in a cross section of older adults, Vitamin D deficiency was associated with low moods and impairment of cognitive performance. [3b]

Fish such as salmon and herring are rich in Vitamin D, as are foods like eggs and ham. Put simply, our mind and body are delicately balanced between energy demand and supply, which means that our rate of thinking, and as we've seen, the quality of those thoughts, can be directly affected by the demands we place on the organs which metabolise energy for the body in general.

Let's take a quick look at one of the most important aspects of this idea, which we in the West tend to overlook, but which is treated very seriously in the Far East.

## THE LIVER

The liver is one of the most important organs in the body, alongside the heart and brain. This majestic workhorse is designed to deliver an impressively long list of functions for our physical well-being, although conventional Western medicine tends to focus on only a smaller sub-section of them. The body depends on the liver to perform a large number of vital functions which can be divided into the following categories:

*i) Cleansing the blood:*

This includes metabolising alcohol, drugs and chemicals and neutralizing and destroying toxic substances by filtering them out of the blood as it streams through the main body of the liver.

*ii) Regulating the supply of body fuel:*

This includes producing, storing and supplying quick energy (glucose and ketones) to keep the mind alert and the body active. It also has a vital role to play in producing, storing and exporting fat, as well as converting these lipids into materials which can be used as energy sources when needed by the body.

*iii) Managing proteins:*

Manufacturing the essential body proteins (lipoproteins) which are involved in transporting crucial materials to repair our cells throughout the body. The liver also helps to regulate the clotting of blood and produces the Kupffer cells which are an important part of fighting infection in the body.

*iv) Managing bile:*

Producing bile which acts as a bactericide, destroying many food borne microbes, and also helps in the digestion of fats in food. Also used to recycle cholesterol.

*v) Managing hormones:*
Regulating and producing hormones such as sex hormones, thyroid hormones, cortisone and other adrenal hormones. These hormones are an essential part of the body's regulatory system.

*vi) Managing cholesterol:*
Regulating body cholesterol by producing it, excreting it, and converting it to other essential substances. Cholesterol is vital for repairing cell material in the body. The liver creates around 25% of our body's total daily cholesterol production (which is around 1g a day).

*vii) Managing vitamins and minerals:*
Regulating the supply of essential vitamins and minerals such as iron and copper.

*viii) Various:*
Performing literally hundreds of other specific functions within the body and metabolic system!

In fact just about everything that we swallow that is absorbed into the bloodstream ends up passing through this amazing organ. As well as being the largest organ in the body it is also the only one which is capable of self regeneration. Whilst there is still much that is unknown about the full functionality of the liver it is fair to say that it is absolutely central to the body's metabolism, or the process by which the living matter in our body is produced, maintained or destroyed. So what does this mean for our thoughts and stress?

## TRADITIONAL MEDICINE AND BEYOND

Bearing in mind the obvious importance of this organ to our overall physical well-being, it is no accident that the ancient practices of Indian Ayurvedic and Chinese medicine place a significant amount of focus on the liver. Its role in keeping the body free of harmful toxins and regulating our hormone levels means that it is clearly a vital link in the interaction of mind and body. This is why it's easy to directly trace its influence in things like the oscillating mood swings caused by fluctuations in our blood sugar levels or hormonal secretions, and its effect on our energy levels through the application of bile to our digestive system. No wonder it is held in such high regard by the medical profession.

*"The liver, that great maroon snail: No wave of emotion sweeps it. Neither music nor mathematics gives it pause in its appointed tasks."* Dr. Richard Selzer, 1976.

There is one area, however, where modern Western medicine deviates from Eastern knowledge, and that is with respect to the significance of heat in the liver. It is generally accepted that the liver generates small amounts of heat as a natural part of its duties in detoxing the bloodstream and synthesizing and breaking down different substances. In fact the blood leaving the liver is known to be marginally warmer than the blood in other parts of the body (except the blood leaving the brain, which also has a significant energy requirement). In normal circumstances this heat is regulated and distributed by the flow of blood through the organ's capillaries – one quart of the five quarts of blood in the human body is filtered by the liver every minute - however if there are significant toxins in the blood or external causes of additional heat on the body, such as heatstroke, then the liver can be damaged through over-heating.[4] Even a mildly over heated liver can cause problems with the body as a whole, as the Chinese and Ayurvedic medical practices acknowledge. [5]

Both Indian and Chinese medicine practices in fact offer specific remedies with which to 'cool down' and heal this important organ.[6] One such herb, for example, gardeniae jasminoidis (zhi zi) - otherwise known as the 'happiness herb' - is renowned for its effectiveness in removing the internal 'heat' which can cause irritability, restlessness and insomnia. In both

Indian and Chinese medicine heat figures strongly in treatments for liverish type problems, and in fact both practices discourage things like eating hot spicy foods and heating foods like red meat, in order to give the liver the chance to 'cool' down.

## THE LIVER AND STRESS

In terms of the connection between the liver and our feelings of stress, it's fairly easy to see that because of the liver's direct connection with delivering energy to the brain via glucose, it can have a direct and fundamental effect on the flow of thoughts that stream through the mind at any one time. It's not so much that the glucose fuels thoughts, but that it provides the kind of conditions that our frantic imaginings may need if we're in the middle of a stressful period in our life.

The clues to this are all around us. We tend to think of liverish people as being red faced and irritable (dissatisfied for no reason?) and we often tell people not to get '*hot and bothered*' or '*hot under the collar*', or even to stop being a '*hot head*' when they're starting to get upset. In general, in almost every culture we'll find that heat is associated with anger, or upset or imbalance of some sort. We also often describe children as 'liverish', and traditional western medicine recognizes the idea of a person being 'colicy' in nature.

So it's hardly surprising then, that we should take note of the liver, which is a significant regulator of heat in the body as we've seen above, as a part of our campaign to remove stress from our lives. Over-burdening our liver with excess amounts of alcohol, caffeine and other drugs (even things like preservatives and colouring agents) means the liver has to work extra hard to clear these toxins, which of course can have a significantly adverse impact on its other functions.

There are also definite effects on our attention from an overheated liver, since a struggling liver will not provide an optimum delivery of fuel to the brain, which means that we're likely to struggle with a fragmented or inconsistent attention, fatigue and other symptoms from time to time. The poor quality of some junk food also perhaps explains the rise in ADHD and other ailments of the attention, since again the poor old liver has to cope with handling all this highly processed garbage at a cost to overall mental balance and stability.

It is a well known aspect of liver disease that patients can also suffer from mood swings, which include depression, poor concentration and particularly increased anger and irritability. It is also important to remember that the most effective medical methods of treating a problematic liver is through improving the diet, cutting out alcohol and doing regular exercise.[7] Regular meditators will often experiment with various techniques to manage the condition of their liver when they feel that it's out of balance. It generally only needs a careful change in their general diet, for example by avoiding caffeine, alcohol, fatty foods, red meat, and overly rich foods etc to reap the benefits of a calmer attention and more serene meditations.

It is also possible to physically evaluate the temperature of the liver, as you can literally feel its heat just by putting your hand on the liver area (the top right hand side of the stomach area). If you feel that it is noticeably warm, then you know that you need to take some action. Drinking a good amount of water each day also helps with the cooling process (and will help to prevent gallstones too), as can cool showers, swimming sessions and even something as basic as placing a store bought ice pack on the liver area during meditation or when the liver area feels particularly warm.

But ultimately nothing helps to soothe down a heated liver condition more than the regular practice of the right kind of meditation.

### REFERENCES
1. http://en.wikipedia.org/wiki/Allostatic_load

2. http://www.rockefeller.edu/research/faculty/labheads/BruceMcEwen/
3. http://physrev.physiology.org/content/87/3/873.long
3b. http://www.ncbi.nlm.nih.gov/pubmed/17138809
4. http://informahealthcare.com/doi/abs/10.1080/003655299750025778
5. http://ayurvedaprograms.blogspot.co.uk/2010/03/ayurveda-and-liver-health-health-of.html
6. http://www.ncbi.nlm.nih.gov/pubmed/10921385
7. http://en.wikipedia.org/wiki/Liver_disease

## NOTES

# - CHAPTER 6 -

## Introduction To Thoughtless Awareness Meditation

What is meditation?

The classical definition of meditation is any practice which regulates the mind in order to enjoy a transcendent form of consciousness. Typically the practice involves sitting in silence, with the eyes closed and the attention directed inside, rather than externally. There are many different forms of meditation, ranging from deeply religious practices which relate to the unity of soul and cosmos, to simple contemplation which aims to relax the body.

## What makes this meditation program different?

There are two key differences between the form of meditation used in this program and other forms you may find elsewhere.

The first is the fact that where other types require you to focus your attention on a specific aspect (e.g. on your breathing, on the present moment, on a mantra or other visualisation), this form of mental silence meditation emphasises the importance of emptying the mind of thoughts as much as possible. Hence the concept of 'thoughtless awareness'.

Before we go any further, it may help here to specify what we mean by thoughtless awareness. We often use the term mental silence as a shorthand for thoughtless awareness, but they are actually subtly different. The key component of the latter is the fact that we are absolutely 'aware' of our surroundings (e.g. noises, smells etc) during meditation. While we can experience mental silence during dreamless sleep and while unconscious, we can only ever enjoy thoughtless awareness during meditation, it is a completely unique and very powerful state. It is a completely different state to visualisation, mindfulness, trance or self hypnosis, and because it is so intrinsically connected to the flow of subtle energies inside us, we are elevated above and beyond our mental apparatus. Our attention literally moves beyond the mind.

Of course it is generally very difficult to stop thinking, since thoughts are a fundamental element of existence, but the second crucial aspect of this meditation is the fact that we do not have to 'do' anything specific to achieve this state of inner silence. Think of it like learning to float in the sea. When we first try, we tend to tense up, and that makes us sink despite our best efforts. But once we learn to lean back into the water in a relaxed state, our natural buoyancy keeps us afloat without thinking about it. It's the same with thoughtless awareness in meditation. In this case, we rely on an in-built system of energies to do the task for us. Specifically we rely on an energy called Kundalini, which can be found in all individuals, typically in a dormant state.

Once we start to meditate, this energy begins to flow through our subtle system, and effects all of the changes we need, including taking us gently into a state of thoughtless awareness, where the flow of thoughts slows down spontaneously and we enter into a zone of peace. The process has to be automatic like this, because in order to achieve a genuine state of peace, we need to move beyond all wilful actions in our mind, otherwise we are merely achieving a state of inner contemplation. In other words it is impossible to go beyond the mind, using the mind. We need some other agency to help us reach the silent oasis.

The idea of tapping into hidden inner energies and seeking to silence the pattern of thoughts without focusing on it may sound far-fetched, and we'll not deny that it can be tricky at first to touch this state, but we know from decades of experience and observation with thousands of practitioners that it can and does work. And in most cases with dramatic results. Another important thing to note about the difference between the search for mental silence and the idea of focusing on a visualisation of some sort as with other practices, is the fact that over time we don't just meditate, we actually become the meditation. That is, our personalities become re-structured internally so that the silence becomes a part of our being.

In fact the meditation itself becomes a living part of our personal growth, and over time guides us towards a generally more balanced way of living. Obviously this is not something that happens overnight, it's a long term process, but the goal is very real, and eventually we will notice fundamental beneficial changes to our patterns of behaviour and personality.

Of course many other forms of meditation also offer benefits, but with thoughtless awareness, the changes are significantly more identifiable and indelible. It is almost as though we spontaneously alter our genetic structure in some way to re-wire our mental and emotional world view, without having to engage in some form of positive thinking or other mental gymnastics. Obviously the pace of change will differ from person to person, as will the impact of the effects over time, however the one thing we do know from experience is if you sincerely have the desire to change and diligently meditate every day, you will experience a profound and automatic shift in the way you live your life in many different and important ways.

Other forms of meditation are rather like top class nutritional diet regimes, which help you lose weight, but are something which you have to 'focus' on all your life. Thoughtless awareness meditation on the other hand is like a fundamental lifestyle change, which operates to effect mental, physiological and spiritual change *automatically* from the core of the personality outwards. Because this change is done outside of the layer of thoughts generated by our ego, it also has the effect of dissolving the typical interactions between ego and superego that people often find so debilitating, especially where stressful events are concerned.

The nearest analogy we can come up with is the difference between learning to ride a bicycle and the effort required when you're proficient at it. During the early days we need to expend a lot of effort and focus on maintaining balance while trying to steer the craft around obstacles. However once we have practised enough, our muscle (or procedural) memory kicks in[1], and we start to cycle automatically with full confidence. We don't 'think' about it any more, because our muscles and sense of balance have become embedded in the process. We can see the same effect with virtuoso musicians who can play incredibly complicated pieces of music from memory without needing to sight read, simply because the pieces have been indelibly imprinted on their minds and bodies through regular and diligent practise.[2]

## HOW CAN MEDITATION HELP MY STRESS?
We have seen above how stress is the direct result of our thoughts and the environmental impacts which affect them, and we have also seen how our noisy lifestyle can also worsen the

negative aspects of our thought patterns when faced with a stressful situation.

The thoughtless awareness meditation used as part of this program in effect acts as a form of microsurgery for the mind, by gradually eroding the negative structures which are created by stressed thought patterns, replacing them with a more benign form of attention which puts a new perspective on our life view in lots of key ways.

The idea is not to repress the negative thoughts - or negative automatic thoughts (NATs) as the cognitive scientists call them - which are creating the stress, but to detox them in the mind, so they become benign components of our overall thought flow. Rather than make repetitive journeys down the imaginary dead end alleys of our fears, anxiety, uncertainty and doubts, we instead acknowledge the facts of the situation, look at them dispassionately and then move on to continue with the rest of our life as part of the process to sort things out.

This ability of regular meditation to dissolve stressful mental reactions happens in two stages. In the first stage we experience a soothing of the stressful reaction during the meditation itself. However in the early days these negative thoughts will inevitably return during the day as the effects of the meditation wear off. But after a period of continual regular meditation, practitioners notice that their overall stress levels start to decrease in general, as the 'microsurgery' starts to disrupt the negative thought patterns which feed the stressful feelings.

This is another of the major differences between this stress relief program and other forms of meditation or positive thinking. While positive thinking can also deliver temporary relief over stressful thoughts, sooner or later they return to intrude and we end up having to engage in a constant battle to suppress them so we can continue with our lives. It's a battle which can be debilitating in itself. Similarly, other forms of commercial meditation do not have the power to significantly change the thought patterns which give rise to the stress, and instead will typically deliver some form of moment to moment diversion from the stress through focused attention or visualisations.

## THE AMAZING ENERGY

As we said above, the key reason why this meditation is so uniquely effective is because true mental silence can only be achieved with the help of an integrated spiritual energy inside us called the Kundalini[3], and it is only through the use of this powerful agent that we can transition into a truly powerful state of thoughtless awareness – i.e. go beyond the mind.

Where programs such as Cognitive Behavioural Therapy help to train the mind manually through focus and control, thoughtless awareness meditation helps our whole personality to transition naturally and automatically into a new, more positive state of being... beyond thought altogether. The process of the meditation is deceptively simple. We sit down, close our eyes with our palms on our lap and take our attention to the top of the head. As we do this, we allow the Kundalini to rise from the base of the spine, up along the path of our spinal column and emerge from the top of the head.

It is actually possible during the meditation to feel this process happening in the body, as a gentle cool flow up the spinal region, or a cool (or warm) flow emitting from the top of the head. In the early days most practitioners spend a lot of time checking this cool flow to verify that the meditation is working properly. It's quite an interesting experiment to conduct, and newcomers to thoughtless awareness are often pleasantly surprised by how much they actually feel as the process works. You may even be feeling something similar as you read this? Heavy smokers may have some difficulty at first, but the signs are a very soft, cool sensation coursing over the palms or up the spine or top of the head.

As the Kundalini energy makes this journey, she heals and clears out any blockages in our subtle system of spiritual centres or chakras,[4] soothes down our ego and emotional conditionings, and brings our whole personality into balance in a very profound way.

We say the meditation is deceptively simple because, while there is a complex interaction of energy flows going on behind the scenes, from our perspective all we experience is the sensation of peace, a slowing of the thoughts and perhaps a few light physical sensations such as prickling on the fingers or coolness on the hands, head or body. There are many techniques we can use to enhance and intensify the experience of this meditation, but for the purposes of this stage of our experimentation it will help if we put these to one side for the moment, and just concentrate on sitting still with our eyes closed and the thoughts gently dissolving in our mind. If we can achieve this, and finish up feeling refreshed, calm and invigorated, we know that our meditation has been fruitful. We'll run through the process in more detail later on.

### THE POWER OF SILENCE

We have already seen just how damaging noise can be to our lives, and in the same way we each hold the power of self-improvement in our own hands. We can continue to battle against our increasingly noisy society or we can step back from the edge and return to the core humanity which gives us an inner peace that rejuvenates. The science already demonstrates the damage that comes from our high octane lifestyles, and while we may make the best of it, deep down we realize that the process is not sustainable in the long run.

One question that you may be asking is why does the cure have to involve *inner* silence? Why can we not just retreat to a physical location where the noise of the modern lifestyle dies away and we gain peace that way? This is certainly an option which many people do take. All around the world we can find reclusive communities, where people drop out of society and revert to living simple lives. However the material simplicity of their lives is often not accompanied by any inner peace, as their minds remain filled with the fears, doubts and confusions of living day to day, in much the same way as their urban counterparts. Personal relationships, character clashes, and factors such as the tension of subsistence living can often create just as much of a noisy mental environment as worries about credit card debt.

It is only when we can free ourselves from the bindings of our mental processes that we can find real peace! The other crucial need for inner mental silence is the fact that it delivers much more than just a cessation of noise. It really is a healing power, and one which can actually elevate us above and beyond the mundane demands and desires of material existence. The whole process of meditation goes much further than just offering us a space to think without distraction. By entering into a zone of thoughtlessness, we encourage a wide range of benevolent forces to act on our physical being too, and so heal our imbalances and ailments.

That's not to say that the meditation can be some sort of miracle medical cure, because that is not how it works. The meditation brings our whole being back into balance, and because of that, our in-built antibodies and immune system can start to work properly, unimpeded by our cluttered mental state and the chemical impediments that those thoughts can generate. The fact is our body is an extremely delicate system of electrical and chemical processes, which all act in cohesion to keep us in a state of physical and mental well-being.

Our extreme and often unbalanced modern lifestyle is directly antithetical to this delicate system, and while we are masters of adaptation, every stress laden signal that we introduce into this system reduces its efficiency and long term stability. By giving our system a silent period every day, we allow it time to redress and repair the imbalance introduced by the interactions of our lifestyle, and so allow for a healing to occur. It's rather like resting the soil between harvests to allow for a replenishment of nutrients.

We shouldn't expect instant cures, or be disappointed when we still catch cold or come down with a nasty bout of flu. There are many instances when our system will be overcome by imbalances and external elements which are too powerful to control in the short term. But those who meditate diligently and regularly should definitely expect to fight off general infectious ailments more efficiently, and also improve the effectiveness of their immune system in general.

Over time we also become a generally more meditative person, and that has huge repercussions on every aspect of our life. We make more intelligent decisions, develop a more astute intuition, make better use of our innate creative powers and in general become a more emotionally intelligent and compassionate personality. All of these benefits come with time, and they will occur in different strengths and flavours depending on the person who is meditating. We all have different temperaments and characteristics and these play out to deliver our own custom progress as we meditate. In the same way that no two fingerprints are the same, so too the journey for each meditator is different.

A quiet, still mind is a mind that also has the time and space to focus on aspects of our lives that a fragmented attention can miss. If we are constantly thinking, reacting to events and generally acting as a puppet of our emotions then we are running at the limits of our consciousness. There is no time for reflection or for the consideration needed for intelligent decision making. We operate almost in auto-pilot mode. Once we discover the power of silence, and through it the ability to quieten our thoughts when they become burdensome, we learn how effective it can be to focus on one stream of attention at a time. Our attention is not fractured by frivolous or trivial distractions, and so we can make fast efficient decisions and move on. We don't waste our thinking and fritter it away, but instead we cherish it and listen more to the quiet internal voice that can guide us to where we need to be.

They say that intuition and creative genius comes from flashes of mental acuity which can occur at any time, but in many cases they come about when we are relaxed and focused on a single goal. It is rare to hear anyone claim they had an inspired idea on a jam packed bus in the morning rush hour, or while in the middle of a heated argument. At those times our mind is working overtime in other directions. Artists tend to experience their best inspiration in the quiet hours of the night or early morning, or on long country walks surrounded by nature.

*'Silence is a source of great strength.'* Lao Tzu

The quiet mind creates its own zone of contemplation within which emotional intelligence has room to expand and thrive. And act. Within this mind, genius, poet and artist co-mingle and ideas flourish. The stillness becomes a fertile breeding ground for wisdom and generosity. We can gain so much from the silence of that inner universe if we allow ourselves time to encourage and embrace it.

## GROWING SELF AWARENESS

Equally important to our well-being is the part that silence plays in the process of our self-awareness. Most of us don't have the time to examine ourselves in any detail during our hectic lifestyles. Those with enough of a reason and a large enough budget may employ psychiatric or counselling help to achieve some measure of understanding, but for the vast majority this is a luxury we cannot afford.

Giving ourselves a set space of silent time each day delivers exactly the kind of environment which stimulates our own personal process of introspection. We extract insights into our behaviour, relationships and desires from the balance that meditation delivers. While the meditation involves mental silence, the fruits of that silence can happen at any time of the day or night, so we can have powerful insightful realisations while we're brushing our teeth, or while brewing a cup of tea.

This process of gently increasing self-knowledge again happens over time and with regular meditation. At times these episodes can be significant milestones in our personal development, and can even be a little surprising in their intensity, but typically they occur as a gentle flow of increased personal understanding over the course of many months and years. Patience is the key to this process. There are many additional aspects of this process of silence in meditation which can enrich our lives. More fruitful relationships, more confidence in abilities and improved efficiency are just a few of the examples of things that people report as they continue to meditate.

We unlearn bad habits, and re-acquaint ourselves with beneficial ones. We avoid the destructive and seek out the constructive whenever we can. We cherish optimism and a fun loving attitude, and refuse to let trivial events upset our sense of balance. But in general this new process of self-improvement helps us realise that we still have the ability to enjoy life, with all its different modes, shades, challenges and peculiarities. We enjoy the participation.

All too often our lives become so complicated and cluttered that we forget how to really enjoy everything that this marvellous existence has to offer. The love, passion, excitement and surprise that await us around every corner. Through meditation and inner silence we rediscover the joy of experience, and what's more we return to a more open and accepting personality. The illusory material happiness we often seek as consolation for our stressed lifestyle is replaced by an appreciation of simple pleasures, and our love of culture and elevating experiences are given a renewed vigour. We wake up to a new passion for life. While this may seem fanciful, it is no more than the result of the focused attention and balance that mental silence brings to our lives.

When we are free from unnecessary fear and open to new experiences, we become a more liberated personality in every way. Our meditation clears out the doubts, petty emotions and blockages which can create barriers to enjoyment, and helps us soak up our life experiences as though with fresh enthusiasm. Our enjoyment of the simple life in turn leads to the kind of freedom we may have been seeking but were unable to find. When our mind is quiet and at peace, we do not need any external stimuli to fill a void, we are content.

Like the deep quiet waters of a still lake, we exist for the moment, with all the pleasure that brings. A core part of the renewed appreciation of life which comes from a regular practice of meditation is discovering that peace really does exist within all of us in a potential state. It is up to each of us to use our inner silence to help it flower. We talk about peace all the time, we award prizes for it, we praise those who deliver it, and yet we find it difficult if not impossible to reliably experience it ourselves.

This is because we have built a civilisation which gives us too few moments of precious tranquillity within which to touch the peace within. Our minds continually race to an unseen drumbeat, and our thoughts constantly drag us into turbulence. But as we've seen, we don't have to be the victim of our thoughts, we can take back control and over time develop the type of mental stability which is powerfully soothing. The peace which comes from meditation is strong enough to quell the noise in our lives and let us exist in a permanent oasis of calm. Unlike drugs or other artificial methods, it does not numb the noise or wall us off in a mental prison, but instead liberates us so we can face the most hectic or traumatic situations and events with an unshakable inner calm and fortitude.

## Two Stages Of The Meditation

There are two distinct stages in the meditation practice.

1. *Practising the meditation.* This is the early stage, where we first learn how to practice the meditation, and master the basic techniques which will help remove the stressful components in our day to day life. The idea is for us to make space every day for a short period of silent meditation which will effect the changes we seek. The key thing to remember about this early period is it's similar to using a sticking plaster on a wound. It will give temporary relief, but in order to obtain permanent relief we will need to move on to a more fundamental process, which is where the second stage comes into play.

2. *Becoming the meditation.* For those who wish to take the process further, this is the stage which provides the long term immunity to the effects of stressful life events. The hallmark of someone for whom the meditation is becoming embedded is a shift in life focus towards a deeper search for self-knowledge and improvement. They become intrinsically more serene and balanced, and their personality changes shape at the core. The key to achieving this change lies in our willingness to surrender to a patient, steady process of self-awareness through meditation. If we genuinely wish to '*vaccinate*' ourselves against the effects of future trauma, we will need to understand ourselves better than we have ever done before. Eventually we will discover new dimensions to our personality that we never imagined, as the meditation gently takes root in our lives.

The best news is this journey is all accomplished through the power of our regular meditation. There's no need for complex tuition or any other form of rigid formality. Just the steady practice of the meditation outlined here, along with a few simple exercises to help the mind become more resilient and stable, and you will be on your way. Treat it as a lifestyle journey, enjoy the process and forget about a destination, and you will reap the rewards you have been seeking.

## THE ROLE OF BALANCE IN MEDITATION

One very important factor which plays a direct role in the effectiveness of our meditation practice is our state of balance. By that we mean how well we manage to maintain a state of equilibrium from day to day. We naturally oscillate across a wide spectrum of emotional states and moods throughout our daily lives. One moment we can be positive and enthusiastic, the next unsure and uncertain. In small amounts these shifts are perfectly normal, as we adjust from circumstance to circumstance. And many of us also develop a natural temperament over time, which can either be more positive or more negative in general, which affects these oscillations.

However during times of stressful or challenging situations these oscillations can become extreme, which means that we move from merely feeling unsure to being anxious, or from feeling enthusiastic to being hyperactive and so on. At the extremes these swings can even become damaging to our health, in terms of impacting our physical state and mental stability.

The stress that comes from hyperactivity, or the depression which arises from, say, uncertainty can deliver real negative impacts on our life. The release of a continued flow of stress related hormones into our body can cause a weakening of the immune system, as well as sheer exhaustion. For example, we often succumb much quicker to coughs and sneezes when we're over stressed because our body's macrophages are weakened by the release of cortisol, a stress related hormone.

Prolonged stress can also affect our ability to manage memories, raise our blood pressure to dangerous levels and deliver ulcers, migraines and other unpleasant effects. By meditating regularly we can take control of these oscillations and help to prevent the worst excesses of any stressful situations from manifesting properly. In effect we damp down the potential problem through our periods of silence in meditation every day. This issue of keeping ourselves balanced every day through our meditation goes further than just preventing the worst of the stressful impacts. We can also start to benefit from an overall sense of self-control and balance in our lives which delivers many more long term benefits. Once we have a stable foundation, i.e. we don't easily find ourselves pushed '*out of sorts*' by general life events, we can start to learn who we really are.

The meditation gives us a stronger foundation from which to manage our relationships as well, which again can help to keep our exposure to stressful situations down to a minimum. In practical terms, this state of balance is automatically delivered every time we sit down to meditate. We don't have to do anything special, the system just resets every time. However in extreme situations, we may find that even the meditation does not calm us down, or lift us up to the degree we need, and in those cases we can use a range of small techniques to help the process along.

For example if we are feeling down, we can help ourselves out of the 'hole' by adding more bright light to our environment. It may sound strange, but our body really does respond to light in ways we cannot explain, which is why many people use SAD (seasonal affective disorder) lights during the darker winter months, to improve their overall moods.[5]

In a similar vein, if we are feeling too 'hyper', we can try and cool ourselves down by staying out of the hot sun as much as we can, or by limiting our intake of heating substances such as fried food, coffee or alcohol. Often taking just these simple steps for a few days can help us restore the balance we've lost, and we'll notice an improvement in the meditation as well. One of the other ways we can help this process is to keep a track of how we're feeling each day to try and track our progress. In a similar vein, the exercises below at the end of the book are designed to help us maintain a stable balanced state for as long as possible. We also provide a simple evaluation checklist in Appendix I to help you keep a log of which side of the balance spectrum you feel at any one time,. By referring to it every week, you'll be able to spot potential problems before they become acute, and deal with them.

If you run through the checklist and find that you're definitely at the 'hyper' end of the scale, you can make adjustments accordingly, both during the meditation and while you go about your daily activities. On the other hand, if you find you're slipping into a more 'down' state, then again you can take corrective action as outlined below. As we said before, many of us actually grow up and mature into our own natural temperament, whether that means we're generally more hyperactive or more mellow reflective personalities, and these tendencies will add to the mix we have to watch out for.

However once again, they can be managed with the help of the checklist and meditation. The important thing is not to worry about the fact that you're not feeling balanced, but to just take the steps you need and wait patiently for the meditation to resolve the issues over time. It may take hours, or it may take days, but the power of the meditation will work if you stick with it.

One of the other interesting aspects to this question of balance is it goes beyond simple issues such as stressed work situations or relationships, and can include things which are as mundane as allowing yourself to become angry and unforgiving over some situation or event. Research[6] has demonstrated that harbouring grudges for a long time can really have a negative impact on your health, in some cases literally with things like blood pressure and heart rate.[7] If you find yourself in this situation, then using the meditation to help dissolve these unharmonious issues will not only keep the stress away, but also help you avoid any negative impact on your physical well-being. This is yet another side-benefit from the meditation that goes beyond simply soothing away our overt stress experiences.

We've only given a very basic outline of the issue of balance through meditation here, but for the purposes of this book it will serve as a useful foundation to start with. The really amazing thing is how quickly we can learn how to monitor and adjust our state of balance through the use of our daily meditation. It really is an incredibly powerful tool for staving off stress and personal mental trauma. Should you want to delve deeper into the subject, you will find out more from www.freemeditation.com, or the site which accompanies this book, MeditationForStress.net, both of which cover the subject in more depth.

There's also a list of resources at the end of the book which you can also use to read up on balance in more detail if you wish. Do remember though, that at the beginning we suggest that you try to avoid over-complicating your meditation practice by trying to 'learn' too much, because it just adds to the thinking we're trying to avoid. Keeping things simple also makes it easier to keep ourselves in a meditative state for as long as possible. Remember that over-thinking things is the reason we're here in the beginning, so no sense in adding more fuel to the fire just yet, eh?

## References

1. http://en.wikipedia.org/wiki/Muscle_memory
2. http://www.moltomusic.com/music-practice-tips/slower-is-faster/
3. http://www.sol.com.au/kor/14_02.htm
4. http://www.freemeditation.com/meditation-basics/meditation-and-chakras
5. http://en.wikipedia.org/wiki/Seasonal_affective_disorder
6. http://pss.sagepub.com/content/12/2/117.abstract
7. http://www.amazon.com/Anger-Kills-Seventeen-Strategies-Controlling/dp/0061097535

NOTES

# - CHAPTER 7 -

## The Three Step Program

The simple program outlined in this book is made up of three distinct steps, which work together to deliver a long term and robust treatment for the causes and symptoms of stress and anxiety. (*see more info and meditation resources at www.meditationforstress.net*)

- **Meditate**
- **Manage Our Attention**
- **Active Surrender**

## Step 1. Meditation

Before we move on to the actual meditation, it is important to note that this proven method of stress rehabilitation connects very strongly with our innate spiritual nature, and so you will need a willingness to explore a possibly new and unfamiliar dimension of your being. This program is based on a very popular form of meditation known as Sahaja meditation.[1] It is easy to grasp, and doesn't require any kind of exotic knowledge. In fact the simpler you keep it, the better. So for now be prepared just to empty your mind of all thoughts, and enjoy the benefits of this simple cure for the battered soul.

The first thing to recognize is the fact that true meditation is achieved through mental surrender and not through positive action. What does this mean? Well, in order to achieve the kind of mental silence we need, we have to completely relax and allow our thinking processes to slow down automatically in order to go beyond the mind. It's a simple equation: the more we think about trying to meditate, the harder it becomes to stop thinking. While this may appear to be something of a Catch-22, we are helped by a number of factors which we'll come back to later.

Nirmala Srivastava - founder of Sahaja Meditation

As we have learned, scientists will tell you that thoughts are a flow of mental images, which are translated through the filter of the 'self'. Of course this dry rational analysis fails completely to explain so much of the mystery of conscious thought, such as emotion, imagination and the source of our 'I-ness'. However despite our rather poor understanding of the real nature of consciousness and the mind, we can all empathize with the idea of a stream or a flow of thoughts going through our head. Because that's what it feels like, doesn't it?

But if we were to ask you to suddenly and completely stop thinking altogether, the result would be in no doubt. We cannot stop thinking. No matter what we do, after a time - milliseconds in fact - a new mental image will intrude into our mind and we'll be off again on another stream. It's inexorable and unstoppable. So how can the secret to a life better lived occur through trying for something so impossible as thoughtless awareness, where thoughts stop and we just 'are'? Actually we don't need to achieve complete and utter mental silence in order for the magic to happen.

Even after we have been meditating for a while - months, years, or even decades – we are unlikely to achieve anything more than a few minutes of mental silence at a time. But it is possible to achieve, and strange as it may seem, these short repeated moments of thoughtless awareness are all we need to deliver the benefits. Sound incredible? Perhaps, but fortunately there is proof in the shape of hundreds of thousands of happy practitioners of this type of meditation to back up these claims. Not only that, there is also a growing literature of scientific studies which demonstrate that mental silence really does work on many different levels.

One of the foremost researchers on meditation, Dr Ramesh Manocha of Sydney Medical School in Sydney University, has been studying meditation – and in particular thoughtless awareness meditation - for over 15 years, and has published many peer reviewed scientific papers on the physical and psychological benefits which come from regular practice.

He has published a book, called Silence Your Mind[1] which contains dozens of case studies and global peer reviewed research results showing how and why Sahaja meditation works so well. One of the crucial things he and the team discovered during their years of research is, it's not the frequency of the meditation, but the number of episodes of thoughtless awareness in meditation that the practitioners experiences every week, that counts when measuring the quality of their lifestyles in general. Those who regularly experience a number of clearly identifiable spots of silence every week during their meditations generally exhibit significantly improved health and emotional benefits in their day to day lives. Silence really works.

*"One of the most surprising things we discovered in our research is it wasn't the frequency of meditation that counted, but how often the practitioners experienced this state of mental silence that really helped improve their mental health",* he explains, *"We were able to spot the difference between those who simply sat still and appeared to meditate and*

*those who actually experience a period of profound silence in their meditation."*[p]

So, it is important to realize that this is not just a theoretical path you are embarking on, but a tried and tested format which will deliver results as long as you are diligent. You will get out of it exactly what you put in. On many different and amazing levels. Another important point to note is the fact that as we continue to meditate, we will gradually become the meditation; i.e. we will become a more meditative and quiet person within. This permanent inner peace will give us more energy, more passion and more focus than we've ever experienced, and all done naturally over the course of time.

### THE MECHANICS OF THE MEDITATION

Before we start with the actual meditation exercise, let's go over some important points.

1. *What are we expecting in meditation?* We will most likely initially experience a general feeling of quiet in our surroundings, a sort of bubble of peace which settles over us as we sit down to start the meditation. This is the first stage.

Following on from that there is likely to be a period where we experience different sensations, cool, heat, prickling on the fingers, sensations in the body, even above the head. These are all normal and should be watched as if from a distance. We don't need to become involved in the thoughts and sensations, just dispassionately watch the flow as it happens. Don't worry about the flow of thoughts in this stage either, just watch them flow in and out of our consciousness without reacting. The final stage of the meditation will be a series of silent periods, where our thoughts either slow to a crawl, or cease altogether for seconds at a time. This is the period when we are in the deepest part of our meditation and we are experiencing thoughtless awareness.

2. *Factors which can affect our meditation*. It should be noted that there are several factors which can affect the quality of our meditation, and which we should remember as part of our regular practice.

★ Location. It is obviously, especially in the beginning, harder to meditate in the middle of a busy train station, than in the seclusion of an isolated mountaintop forest glade. Eventually both locations will be irrelevant to the quality of your silence, but initially we recommend that you try and choose a quiet spot in your home which you can return to regularly in order to make it easier to meditate as a beginner.

★ Circumstances. There will be days when you sit down to meditate and your whole attention is settled and you find it easier to slip into the peace than normal. Usually these will be when you have few distractions or pressures intruding from your life. On other occasions you will sit down to meditate and the pressures, plans, problems and sheer hassle of life will instantly sit on your head, defying your attempts to feel any sort of peace. Don't despair, just be patient and the peace will come, after a while. Adjust your expectations and prepare to stay with eyes closed for a slightly longer time.

★ Physical. It is incredibly hard to meditate properly when you are in pain or suffering from some other physical ailment such as a cold or flu. The mind will constantly drift towards the source of the problem, and make it extremely difficult to surrender to the silence. In these cases we just have to do the best we can, and realize that just by sitting down to meditate we are helping our healing process to occur, even if it doesn't feel like it. Once the physical issue has passed we will then be able to return to our regular peaceful practice. Even with the distraction of the pain, we must be diligent enough to sit down every day to meditate. It helps the healing and maintains your momentum, so it's vital not to give up.

* Collectivity. We are collective beings, no matter what we may think about the age of the individual. This means we are affected by what happens to our community, our nation and our globe. More than we think. We should not be surprised therefore if our meditation is less than easy on the morning of a major global catastrophe or disaster. In a similar vein, meditating during times of international revelry such as the Christmas period is generally harder than normal because you're effectively surrounded by a multitude of fragmented consciousnesses all focused on different aspects of planning or enjoying. Welcome to your new spiritual world!

3. *What is the goal of each meditation?* What do we want or need to achieve from each meditation? For one, we want to emerge from the experience feeling refreshed, alert, dynamic and totally at peace with our environment. We want to feel rejuvenated, both physically and mentally, with aches and pains gone away and any mental disturbances banished into the ether. But most of all we want to experience silence in a most profound way, even if it's a fleeting encounter at first, because the silence delivers all the benefits. Without the gentle wash of thoughtless awareness across our consciousness we will not enjoy the benefits of the meditation as we need and desire.

So to the meditation itself. Please don't feel you have to follow the suggestions below slavishly. They are there as a guideline, a prop to help you stay on track during the early period of the program. So now let's work our way through the stages and exercises to help experience this process of meditation in a real and tangible form.

## PREPARATION

The very first thing we need to do is re-establish a powerful connection with our attention. The attention is our focus, and as we have seen every day it is battered from all sides by noise pollution and sensory overload.

To meditate properly we need to allocate a space and a time when we can put aside all of these destructive distractions and focus on ourselves, on the inner spirit of our being from which everything comes. We don't need to run off to a mountaintop or hide in a noise-proof chamber, but we should try and find somewhere that is ours, that can be relatively private and quiet and available for us whenever we need it.

We don't have to adopt any particular posture or sit in a lotus position, we should just sit as comfortably as possible, on a chair, sofa, floor or wherever is suitable. It helps to light a candle and have it in front of our position, and if it's available we can make use of natural scenes such as gazing at nature through a window, to help us soothe down the attention as we move into the meditative state. You may also find it easier to meditate if you use incense and/or gentle soothing music playing softly in the background. We have free music available on www.meditationforstress.net which you can listen to if you wish. You will find the tracks, plus other resources under Meditation Tools.

Once we close our eyes, we can also gently draw our right hand up the front of the body from the base of the torso up to the top of the head tracing the path of the Kundalini along the spine. We can do this three or four times to help ourselves move the attention inside. We are also in effect actively demonstrating our desire for the Kundalini to rise and take us into the meditative state. We can also press down on the top of the head with the right hand to help anchor our attention at the top chakra, and then return our hand back down to the lap to continue the meditation in stillness.

Those meditating for the first time may find it difficult to sit still or take their attention inside as they close their eyes, but this does get easier with practice, and there are a couple of simple tricks we can use to help make it easier to go into meditation. For example, if we are feeling overly agitated, just sitting quietly in a dim lit room or a shady location can help cool down our right side energies and move us more into balance before we start. Similarly if we are feeling out of balance through being somewhat depressed or tired, we can improve matters by sitting in a well lit room or in bright sunshine for our meditation. We have also included in Appendix II of this book a set of optional silent affirmations you can use to help take your attention inwards as you start the meditation session.

## THE SESSIONS

It may help to think of each meditation as being split into three parts: Settling, Clearing and the Stillness.

\* Settling

The traditional view of someone in meditation is a person with eyes closed, crossed legged on the floor and with their hands outstretched on the knees and the fingers gently curled. But far more important than this position is the condition of our mind as we enter into a meditative state. We will inevitably suffer from a rush of thoughts as we try and settle into meditation, and we should not try to fight them. On the contrary the challenge is to accept them as a natural part of our meditation, and treat them as the temporary distraction they are.

When we are in the early moments of our meditation, we are trying to settle our mind, take it away from the mundane, and surrender to the loving embrace of the gentle Kundalini energy. Depending on our state of being, we can either be experiencing a rush of thoughts or a dull, lethargic stream, both of which can be frustrating for anyone trying to relax. The good news is that this stage doesn't last long, and if we can remain calm and dispassionate and just watch the thoughts as they occur and disappear, we will soon move into the next stage of the meditation.

**Note**: *This is extremely good training for our attention in general, not only in meditation but in our day to day lives as well, as we will see below. Eventually we'll find ourselves using this technique to stay calm in troubled moments in life, and it will be a fantastic help in those circumstances.*

**Exercise**

There are a number of steps we can take to help ourselves move gently through the settling phase. First we can try and keep our attention at the top of our head as much as possible. Every time we notice our attention wandering to follow a thought or drift off to a noise or external disturbance, we can bring it back to the top of the head, gently and calmly.

Another trick we can use is to fall back on an ancient technique, which although tarnished by movie clichés is actually incredibly powerful. The Sanskrit word '*Om*' (actually AUM, but typically pronounced in the West as OM) has a powerful vibration which immediately triggers a more meditative state when uttered softly and with feeling from the heart. We shouldn't over-use it, but in moderation it's a great way to start the meditation. Just say it to ourselves slowly and silently three or four times. We can also use another Sanskrit language tip, and say silently to ourselves the mantra, '*Neti*' (pronounced '*nayti*')several times. This word means '*not this*', and again has a powerful effect on our thinking process if said a few times silently in our mind, while we keep our attention at the top of our head.

* Clearing

After some moments we should begin to notice that our thoughts are settling down nicely, and we are moving into a more peaceful state. At this point we are on the second leg of our search for the silence that will heal us, and so all we need to do is allow ourselves to dissolve into the peace and surrender to the deepening meditation. We will probably experience thoughts drifting in and out of our mind, but if we maintain our attention at the top of the head then we can stop them dominating us. The key to this stage in the meditation is to keep from doing anything mentally active that could trigger more thoughts, so a gentle use of the '*Neti*' mantra can be useful to stop ourselves succumbing to thought streams. By the time we reach this point, most of the work is being done automatically by the Kundalini, so all we have to do is relax and let it occur. The Kundalini will be extending the space between thoughts, and the state of our chakras and subtle system will determine how hard or easy this is to achieve. If we have been diligent in meditating regularly, then our system is likely to be in robust condition and it will be easier for the silence to sweep across our mind.

*__Note__: This is the stage which can be most frustrating for a beginner, because no matter how hard we try there are days when our thoughts simply won't go away. Especially if we are in the middle of a stressful situation of some sort. The key here is to be patient, both with yourself and with the meditation. Don't give up and stop meditating, give it at least 10 to 15 minutes even if you think nothing is happening. Because it is actually working!*

**Exercise**

It helps at this point if you try not to establish any preset time limit for your meditation, but allow it to continue for as long as you need. A good clue as to whether you have done enough is whether you feel a slight cool sensation on both hands. If you only feel it on one or other hand, then you may need to balance more. However if both hands are equally cool this indicates that your subtle system is in balance.

We may also experience a number of other sensations at this time, such as a subtle sensation of peaceful satisfaction or a gentle feeling of joy which sweeps over you like a wave. Not everyone experiences these feelings in this way, but even a slight exposure to this kind of experience can indicate how well the meditation is going.

★ Stillness

Now we have reached the final stage of the meditation and at this point we may be feeling a profound quiet, coolness from the fingers and palms of the hands and maybe from the top of the head. Thoughts will still be ambling across our mind, but every so often they will cease completely and we will be in another dimension of being. Don't be upset if these periods are frustratingly short, what's important is you experience them over a period of time during your meditation.

Your breathing will have automatically slowed down, and physical distractions will have faded away into the background. Don't succumb to mental clock watching, surrender yourself to the cosmic timer, and let yourself flow with the gentle power of the Kundalini. There's no need to do any visualization or mental gymnastics to improve the experience, just allow it to happen, and keep returning the attention to the top of your head if thoughts return to be a problem.

**Exercise**

In this final stage of our meditation we are in the flow, time has slowed down, our senses are all focused inwards and even though we can still clearly hear external noises and experience smells etc., we are firmly into our zone of peace. The key exercise here is to relax into the meditation and allow the peace to permeate into every part of your being. We can take note of the state of cool in our hands, and see if both palms are cool which is signs that we are in balance. Overall we should try not to focus on anything at all except keeping our attention at the top of our head, to allow the thoughts to drift and dissolve away in our mind.

### Finishing the meditation

There is no set length of time for the meditation, although most people find that between 15 and 30 minutes is adequate for achieving a state of balance. Any less and you don't give yourself enough room to settle into the zone. Once you have been meditating for a while, you may wish to spend longer in the final stage, and so eventually you may even find that an hour has passed quite easily in a delicious state of peace. You will quickly find your own optimum time, so it's not something to worry about. Far more important is the fact that you should meditate regularly and also experience at least some moments of mental silence before you finish, because that is the hallmark of a balanced and beneficial session. The end of the meditation should be accompanied by a slow opening of the eyes, and rather than jumping up immediately, we should stay sitting silently for a few moments to allow the meditative mood to dissipate slowly and naturally.

**Note**: *A useful trick is to try and keep our attention at the top of the head for as long as possible, even after we have our eyes open and we're starting to run through the chores of the day. One way to do this is to again slowly raise the right hand from the base of the torso to the top of the head, following the path of the Kundalini along our spine. Just rest the hand on top of the head for a few seconds after and try and keep our attention locked to that place as we return our hand to our lap.*

The longer we can keep the attention stable like that, the more intensely we will feel the balance throughout our day to day activities. It can even help to try this technique when you're in a completely non-meditative environment, just to see if you can subdue the chatter in your mind and touch some serenity. Try it in a meeting or on the bus and see what the results are. You might be surprised.

Finally, the one thing that will determine how much you receive from your meditation is how much you put into it. Not in effort, but time. To get the best out of your practice you must meditate every single day, first thing in the morning before breakfast, and last thing before you go to bed at night. The evening meditation can be shorter, as it is really to help you sleep, but the morning meditation is the important one. It is not something to obsess about, but rather like forgetting to clean our teeth, if we miss a meditation we will notice the difference, and if we repeatedly miss the sessions then we will definitely lose the benefits. Much better to try and do a little each day than miss out and try to catch up!

## STEP 2. MANAGE OUR ATTENTION

This second part of the stress management process involves a little more day to day effort on our part, as it is a process which spills out into our everyday lives as we go about our business and pleasures. We have already seen how our lifestyles and environment act together to fracture our attention in this modern hectic world, so while the meditation will definitely soothe away the jagged edges of our mind, it is important that we try and maintain our softened attention throughout the day as much as possible.

Luckily, although it sounds hard, there are tips and tricks we can use to make it easier. The idea is for us to keep watch during the day for those danger signs when we are being drawn into a stressful frame of mind, and take action to retreat to a more balanced peaceful state. We can do it, we just need to be vigilant, and once we have practised the techniques a little, we will find that it's quite easy to do. The first thing is to start the day right, so our attention begins as it should continue. We can easily do this by trying to ensure that when we wake up in the morning, we do not immediately assault our senses with too much noise, especially before we have meditated. So we can avoid talking too much, resist the desire to listen or watch the news, or read the newspapers, in fact any action which is likely to excite our mental processes.

Once we have meditated, we will at least have settled our attention into a more stable state, and so we can continue our day as usual without being too overzealous about maintaining the mental silence. However, there may be moments when we find ourselves suddenly faced with something which triggers an attack, and it is then we can use one simple trick to avoid being sucked into a stress attack. Just stop and take the attention immediately to the top of our head. It may sound strange, but that one simple action, can provide immediate relief from any chaos or other turbulent situation, and give us a zone of peace within which to operate. There's no set time limit on the process, usually just a minute or two will be enough, but it should work wonders to soothe the environment, in and out.

Managing the attention doesn't just mean reacting to stressful situations, it also involves actively avoiding potential problems before they happen. If we know we're going to be meeting with someone who is known for their hot temper, or we're in a tense meeting, or even if we're going to have lunch with a friend we know is depressed for some reason, we can take action to avoid being impacted by the situation even before it occurs.

The trick here is again to take the attention inside, and if we can, to the top of the head. It also helps to remember that the situation we are facing (or about to face) can only overwhelm us if we allow our mind to take control. By mentally preparing ourselves, we effectively prevent this happening, by stepping back from the scenario before it happens, and so detach our emotions from any potential issues. By maintaining our inner peace, and keeping our attention under control, we are able to stay calm no matter what happens, which means we don't emerge from the situation frazzled and disturbed.

We can maintain this control of our attention all through the day in these ways, and should try and stay in this calm state before we retire for the night. If you can spare the time, it really helps to enjoy a footsoak before bed (see Appendix III), where we put the feet into a bowl of water (with a pinch or two of ordinary salt in it) before we do our evening meditation. Even 10 minutes of this will help us sleep more soundly at night.

## Step 3. Active Surrender

The final step involves something we call '*active surrender*', which is probably the trickiest aspect of the program to get to grips with. Our meditations over time will help to make our lives more generally balanced, where we feel like we're working with life rather than against it. But sometimes, during times of extreme stress, even with the regular meditation it is possible we will feed trapped at certain moments, maybe even unable to cope. At these times we need to again step back and understand that we don't need to take immediate action to correct the situation, but instead we can relax and let things play out.

This is similar to having faith that things will work out for our particular situation, which is very easy to say, but often very hard to do. Strangely enough, there are times when inaction is definitely the better path to take, to allow things to develop instead of trying to take pre-emptive action. This is the surrender part of Step Three.

### Detachment, surrender and reaction

The key component of our personal surrender to the flow of life comes from a growing detachment from challenging situations. As we continue to meditate, we build a powerful sense of perspective about the difference between the important things in life such as love, respect, truth and ethical behaviour, and less on the ultimately unsatisfactory search for things like power, fame and fairytale romance.

By establishing an inner sense of dispassionate observation, we can really see how to avoid unnecessary anguish by not reacting to every little thing that flitters across our attention. We start to understand how to take advantage of this amazing flow of life, to keep ourselves in balance at all times. This detachment also helps us to avoid becoming fatalistic, or giving up on life because we feel helpless. By being actively surrendered, we continue moving forward in whatever we're engaged with, but we're not overwhelmed with an unhealthy all-consuming desire for any particular outcome. So for example, if we are moving house and there's a delay in sorting out some important aspect of the paperwork, our first instinct is to rush around trying to fix things immediately, at which point our stress levels rise and all the turbulence hits us again.

Perhaps at a time like this, we might instead step back, go make ourselves a cup of tea, try and finish off some other chores and just give the situation a time to settle. Later on we may in fact have to take decisive action, but by leaving things for a while, we give our subconscious time to assimilate the information and perhaps come up with a more elegant way to fix the issue, or accomplish things in an alternative way.

By encouraging this attitude of detached effectiveness, we will notice that even more possibilities open up to us. A similar situation may arise where we are suddenly faced with a surprising, unexpected or maybe even shocking situation. In these circumstances it would be so easy to immediately react, but after we have been practising meditation for a while we will find that we don't. In fact the calm we obtain from our regular meditation helps to take us away from the impulsive reaction to life events which can be a cause of distress and anxiety.

Note that this is not a form of emotional repression, but a genuine mellowing of our typical urge to react to everything that happens to us. In effect we develop a natural 'slow fuse' with respect to action and reaction. This quality is typically one of the hallmarks of people we consider to be 'stable' characters, and we always admire their solidity when we encounter it. These are the traits of someone who is relied upon for advice and guidance in times of trouble, and it is the combination of their detachment and considered wisdom that generally makes their opinion so respected and powerfully effective in times of trouble and unpleasant situations.

### Patience as a virtue

One of the things that science still really doesn't understand is the working of the subconscious, but even so we know it can be an incredibly powerful force in our lives in many ways. Creatively, inspirationally and beyond. So it's strange that we give it so little time to work on things on our behalf. It's a skill we seem to have lost nowadays, although our ancestors definitely used it. Have you ever heard the expression, '*let me sleep on it*'? This was their way to allow solutions to percolate through the subconscious and deliver an answer which was more measured than impulsive. Once we start to meditate active surrender returns that sort of power to our lives, and we're all the richer for it. It is again a part of the same tapestry which gave us the Serenity Prayer from the early 20th century and which has been used so successfully to date in places like the AA meetings for recovering alcoholics around the world.

*'God, grant me the serenity to accept the things I cannot change, the courage to change the things I can, and wisdom to know the difference.'*

This subtle discretion is a hallmark of emotional intelligence, and one of the things that marks out the wise from the weak in many cases. There are so many examples like this where haste is equated with ineptitude ('*fools rush in…*') that it's surprising to see how often we routinely force ourselves to move faster than we probably should, to get things done…chop chop. However by surrendering outcomes and taking a more measured approach to situations we gradually build up our innate detachment and so avoid being consumed by stressful situations. It's an incredibly powerful ability.

Just in case we're accused of being unrealistic with regard to this kind of attitude (surrendering to a raging fire may not be sensible in anyone's book!) it may help to point out that we can still seek to achieve important milestones while adopting this approach. Those who have experienced severely stressful situations will know that one of the most debilitating parts is the feeling of helplessness, when we can't seem to do anything to deliver a positive outcome. And in some cases there are no positive outcomes available to us at all. However even in these cases we can still take action to maintain our mental stability. We can establish milestones and target dates by which even tiny actions should be accomplished, or we can establish a schedule of action, almost like ticking a box a day for example, in order to feel that we're still engaged in the issues and progressing things. There are any number of ways we can still be 'practical' while stepping back from the problem and staying detached from specific outcomes.

We may end up realising that it's not **that** important if a due date isn't met, and that a delay can actually be acceptable. In the same way we may be content to accept a less than optimum outcome if it moves things along more efficiently, and so on. By detaching ourselves from the stressful element of any situation we change from being a steel rod to adopting the powerful flexibility of bamboo. We replace the risk of shattering with an ability to bend with the wind. Think about which one should be more effective in the long run. By following these three basic steps in all our daily dealings, we underpin the work done in our meditations and make the result much more robust. Instead of meditating and then rushing out to meet the day head-on, we adopt a more measured gait, and navigate carefully and gently through the river of events that face us. We become stronger because of it in every way. If we allow ourselves the chance, we can use detachment, surrender and a managed attention to take us to places we could never imagine.

### REFERENCES
1. http://www.sahajameditation.com
2. http://www.amazon.co.uk/Silence-Your-Mind-ebook/dp/B009DIXASO/

NOTES

## NOTES

# - CHAPTER 8 -

### Practical Seven Week Exercises
(*Note: Meditation guides, music resources and other material are available for free on our companion website at http://www.meditationforstress.net*)

Now that we have the basic components in place, we can start to assemble a structured program of weekly exercises based around our regular daily meditation and the three steps, which should help to dissolve stress from our lives. There's no secret sauce, just diligence and a willingness to be flexible in our approach to life. We suggest that you refer to the Balance Checklist at the start of every week (see Appendix I below) to help orient yourself with your general state of balance as you go. The process takes a minute or two, but may help to clarify things and help you to improve your meditations day by day.

### ★ Week One – Introduction
*Goal: To spend the week becoming familiar with the sensations from your daily meditation*

The very first week of your practice should be spent learning about the meditation and what you experience each day as you try for thoughtless awareness. You may already be feeling sensations in and on various parts of your body as you sit down to meditate and it may be helpful to put them into context here.

The first weeks of practising meditation can be a confused whirl of sensations, as we enter into a new world of inner contemplation and silence. We should however, quickly be able to single out particular sensations that we feel as we meditate and also go about our daily routines. For one thing the first thing most people notice is the calming effect that sitting silently delivers. It's as if the brain suddenly has the space it needs to repair and refresh itself, while in a fully working state (as opposed to sleeping, which obviously delivers another type of refreshment during the night).

This general sense of calm can be fleeting or irregular, it doesn't matter in the beginning, just as long as we learn to identify it, since it's the result we are seeking to improve and deepen over time. Take note of how you feel just before you meditate and also just after, and compare your feelings at various points during the day to build a pattern of understanding you can refer to. It may help to keep a small notebook on you, or use your smartphone to track these sensations to see how things are progressing over time. There are other sensations which should be noted as well. For example, when meditating can you feel any coolness or tingling around or inside the body or extremities? These are tell-tale signs that the meditation is working, and your energy system is slowly adjusting to the new force of your meditation.

### * Week two – Silent
*Goal: To spend the week with as little noise as possible.*

The first weeks after we start meditating can be extremely profound in many ways. It's sometimes called the Honeymoon Period because it may be the first time you have ever devoted serious attention to your own deep seated well-being, and your whole personality seems to flower because of that. However we're still regularly assaulted by noise, stress and the cares of the day. This is perfectly natural, and it would be silly to pretend that a single meditation in the morning can change that fact. But as we said at the start, over time you can become immune, or at least greatly protected, from the worst of the turbulence.

The important thing is to give it time, and especially during the early days and weeks to try and keep your attention on silence, even in the midst of the noise. So for example, instead of putting on the radio or TV full blast after you have finished your meditation, just leave it off while you go about the rest of your morning. Try and keep the silence going for as long as you can, internally even if it's not possible externally, with preparing children for school, or yourself for work.

The same applies during the day. For the first week of your meditation practice, try not to talk too much, or let your attention be swallowed up by frivolous things. See if you can maintain some sort of distance from the events happening around you, without seeming to be too strange of course! Make time during the day to just sit silently. Read a book instead of the newspaper or watching TV. Take control of your attention, and if you can, try returning it to the top of your head to see if you can recreate the peace you experience in the meditation.

This kind of exercise is a great way to practice balance, and to establish some sort of internal zone where you can return if and when things start becoming frantic around you. Nobody is suggesting that you wander around in some Zen like state of serenity, that's hardly likely during your first week, but there will be opportunities for you to retreat inside yourself to get some rest, even at work, and you should grab those moments when you can. The result is that by the end of the week, you should be able to say that at least on one or two days you managed to restrain your attention and restore some serenity to your mind even when things were going crazy in and around your environment.

#### How does our meditation help?
Hopefully by now we will be experiencing some sort of peace in our meditation, even if we can only grab fragments of thoughtless awareness during the time we're meditating. During these early weeks, we're going to have to be patient as our system starts to adjust to regular periods of motionless, while our mind rebels a little.

By keeping silent or as quiet as we can be during the week, we can make this adjustment less of a struggle. In effect we are helping ourselves to transition into our daily meditation more easily. The crucial thing is to keep our meditation regular, because the morning meditation sets the tone for our day, and the evening meditation helps us sleep better and awake more refreshed. If we can maintain this virtuous circle twice a day, we will start to notice the effects pretty quickly.

The two main things that our meditation will deliver in these early days is first, the ability to identify our attention with more accuracy. Once we are forced to take our attention inside during a meditation, we can clearly see how it can be fragmented during the day through general activities.

And because we can now recognise the difference, we can take steps over the days and weeks to ensure that we maximise the benefits of the meditations as much as we can. Do not be afraid to keep tabs on your attention at all times through the day, because it will help. And in the same way, make use of the silence in your meditation to understand how powerful and healing the introspection can be.

We are in effect trying to train the mind to respect and enjoy (in fact relish) the new state of peaceful inner contemplation. This will probably be a completely new experience for your mind, and so it will benefit from your gentle but determined approach to the whole process of take more control of your attention. In this way you will be slowly building your mental and emotional resilience and stamina.

## WEEKLY LOG

*Keep a simple log of your week's activities and give yourself 5 points a day for every day when you manage two silent episodes or more. Give yourself 50 points if you manage it every day of the week.*

## ★ Week Three – Slow
*Goal: To take control of the pace and flow of your life.*

Hopefully we will have noticed a distinct, if subtle difference from the episodes we experienced in our Silent week. We may have noticed that our mind seems more restrained, less frantic. Or that our quiet periods are not spent worrying as much as we used to. It's not that we're suddenly magically transformed into Zen like beings who can ignore all emotional trauma, it's just that we have taken one small step along the road to a peaceful mind. Keep it up. Don't forget how powerful silence can be in your life, so make sure you keep watching out for opportunities when you can continue training your mind to sit back and become quiet.

Now for the 2nd week we are going to focus on another important aspect of stress reduction, and that is how we approach the pace of our life in general terms. We live in a time where faster is typically considered to be better. We resort to 'fast food', we look for 'time saving' devices which will do things quicker for us, we applaud athletes who continue to break records in pursuit of faster times.

Much of the focus of our modern world today is on how we can do things quicker to save time, with the implication that all of this 'saved time' will be put to use at some indeterminate period in the future when we can enjoy it. And yet, inexplicably, we don't seem to get any opportunity to take advantage of this spare time. In fact, bizarrely, the faster we run, the less time we seem to have. We commonly suffer what we call 'time poverty', which sums up our current inability to catch up with the demands of an every faster pace of life.

The situation has become so acute for some that there's even a Slow Movement[1] which has been formed to explore and encourage a return to a more sedate way of living. The Slow Movement aims to address the problems caused by 'time poverty,' and help us return to a more connected and balanced lifestyle. The movement is officially described as:

'[A] cultural revolution against the notion that faster is always better. The Slow philosophy is not about doing everything at a snail's pace. It's about seeking to do everything at the right speed. Savoring the hours and minutes rather than just counting them. Doing everything as well as possible, instead of as fast as possible. It's about quality over quantity in everything from work to food to parenting'

This concept of doing everything at the right speed is at the heart of this week's goal. In order to regain our balance and restore some calm to our over-burdened brain, we need to take a step back and evaluate how we progress through each day. How much time do we expend in simply enjoying a particular moment, whether it's listening to music or washing the dishes? The idea of slowing down the pace of our life does not mean that we should become indolent and lazy, but that we should try to take a more measured approach to the way we live day to day. So for the week when we focus on slowing the pace of our life, we should emerge from each morning's meditation with a determined approach to enjoying each moment of that day.

This means that we approach our day with a wish to do things deliberately and with full attention, instead of trying to cram in as many tasks and goals as we can into our activities. Of course we don't all have the luxury of being able to make decisions about the pace at which we do our job, and we're not suggesting a rebellion against the boss, but there are small wins that we can gain from adopting a more measured approach.

Part of it comes from establishing priorities. Which of the day's or week's goals are absolutely essential to our life at that time, and which can be re-scheduled to allow us more space to enjoy? Which task at work is crucial to retaining our livelihood, and which can be safely delegated or shared so that we can focus on the important aspect of our goals for the day? Do we have to fill every minute of our days with a constant flow of activities, or are there some we can genuinely remove or defer? By focusing on the real immediate needs of our lives, we may be surprised to see how much of our time is spent on tasks which actually are not as essential as they seem. And more importantly, we may find that we can adjust our day to the extent that we start to enjoy moments of peaceful reflection and togetherness with friends and family that deliver far more deep seated satisfaction than we thought.

More importantly, by focusing on the small things in life, we can spend less time worrying about future or past events and enjoy the present moment more fully. By spending the week consciously slowing down our activities and goal demands, we learn how to also subconsciously slow down our desires, thoughts and potential stress triggers. We stop worrying about filling our timetable with successful outcomes and instead focus on appreciating all the outcomes of the week, no matter how banal.

Why should we only take pleasure in art, food and the so-called 'leisure' pursuits, when in fact the whole of life has the capacity to deliver equal amounts of joy? Ask anyone who has recently escaped from a life threatening situation and they will confirm that they suddenly realise how much the simple things in life mean to them[2]. This realisation is a crucial milestone on anyone's journey for a calmer, more satisfying life, and if we can start to encourage this mental attitude right at the beginning of our journey of meditation, we will be all the better for it.

The Slow Movement now encompasses a wide range of human endeavours, including Slow Art, Slow Food, Slow Media and Slow Parenting, which aims to help encourage parents to step back a little from 'hyper-parenting' and allow their children the space to grow without added pressure from parental expectations. We encourage you to allow a little (or a lot) more slow into your life, you may be surprised by how much of a benefit it delivers over the long term.

## How does our meditation help?

The success of the goals this week depend to a large extent on your personal circumstances. If you're a busy executive in a large city, juggling multiple responsibilities at home and work, it will obviously be more difficult to adopt a more sedate mode of activity. This is where your meditation should really help however.

By starting your day with a solid meditation, we should be able to identify areas where we can in fact adjust our pace without causing upheaval. There is a school of thought which says that it is not the large gains which determine success, but the tiny improvements, and this is very true at this stage. See here[3] for an example of what we mean. Even a 1% reduction in the pace at which you operate during a busy schedule, a slightly longer lunch break, an hour spent walking in the park at the weekend rather than finishing a work task, and so on. Look for the tiny incremental opportunities, and don't worry if you don't think it's enough. Over time it will be.

During this period your meditation will be the rock on which these small gains rest. For one thing, because of your meditation, you will start to enjoy the challenge of finding small wins during your day. Your meditation opens up a whole new world of reality, in other words the joy of the simple, rather than the constant race for the illusory. Once this process is set in motion your live will start to change in imperceptible but key ways. You will emerge from each day's meditation a little more able to ignore the trivia and deal with what's really important in your life. Like relationships and the joy of the now.

## Weekly Log

*Keep a simple log of your week's activities and give yourself 5 points for each day when you manage to genuinely take conscious control of your activities to encourage a slow day. Give yourself 50 points if you manage it every day of the week.*

## ★ Week four – Centered

*Goal: To spend the week enjoying the present moment as much as possible.*

Another aspect of our lives which is allied very closely to the speed at which we live, is the fact that we typically find it very difficult, if not impossible, to focus our attention on the present moment. In fact, if we analyse our mental process throughout a typical day, we'll find that almost all of our thoughts relate to either the future or the past. Which explains a lot of the anxiety and frustration that can build up about one situation or another. The past is gone and we cannot change it at all. We may be able to take actions to mitigate or reduce any distressing aspect of the past, but we can't alter what happened at all. In the same way, we have no power to alter or affect what's going to happen in the future.

Of course we can make plans to try and deliver one effect or another, but we have no way of knowing if these plans will come about as we expect or hope, or whether some unforeseen $3^{rd}$ party or event will scupper our plans completely. This uncertainty – and impotence - is one of the most fundamental causes of the root distress we feel from unpleasant situations, and the longer we spend going over and over the same options again and again, the worse it gets. We've already talked about woulda, coulda, shoulda, but this frustrating, ineffective feeling seems to act as an amplifier to any upset we feel, and in fact makes it 100 times worse in our mind.

The object of this week's exercise is to corral the attention and force ourselves to focus on the present moment as much as possible. At first this will be incredibly difficult, so don't expect miracles from day one, but over time, the meditation and your general more open attitude will help you to bring about quite significant alterations to the way you approach your life, moment by moment. The first trick to making this goal achievable is to learn what it feels like to have your attention on the present moment. The best athletes and musicians know the feeling well, as in their circles it's known as 'flow'. This state, which is in effect a form of mental silence in meditation, as first described by Professor Mihaly Csikszentmihalyi is '*a feeling of energized focus...and a complete absorption in what one does*'.[4]

Flow is used by athletes to give them an added edge in their competition, but absorbing oneself in the present moment is equally effective in helping us mitigate the effects of stressful situations. It's surprising how hard it is for negative thoughts to intrude into our consciousness when we're actively focusing on the now. Just the mere fact that we direct our full attention onto an activity is enough to keep ourselves in a more calm state.

Of course it's almost impossible to maintain this focus for anything more than a few minutes at a time, unless we're engaged in running a 400 meters dash, but we can definitely use the meditation to help train our minds in how to achieve a more successful mental silence, which defines the here and now. We can also make use of the tips we use in meditation to stay in the present, by putting our attention on the top of the head, keeping it there as long as possible, and by perhaps sometimes using the '*Neti*' mantra, to bring our thoughts back into some control.

This goal is something that can be challenging, especially if we're busy at work, and expected to make decisions about the future and past from minute to minute. In these circumstances we're clearly going to have to deal with the demands of the job and that probably won't allow for much time to try and establish something as tricky as a controlled mental focus. However even in these situations we should be able to find moments when we can drop out of the immediate environment, and instead of day-dreaming (as we might do, say, in a boring meeting) spend them by focusing our attention on what is happening right now; where we are sitting, the light on our pen, the sound of a speaker's voice and other aspects of that particular moment.

This is not supposed to be an escapist exercise, but instead is intended to help us learn how to manage our attention in a very direct way. It may seem silly and unrewarding, but in the same way that working out in a gym eventually delivers a set of newly developed muscles, so too, practising this type of mental control will lead to the ability to remain calm in the most volatile and traumatic situations. With the meditation as the foundation, this is a solid part of the immunisation process which will stand the test of time.

#### How does our meditation help?

As we progress and our experience in meditation deepens, we will notice how the focus of our lives starts to return to the simple things, rather than the grandiose. Because of our new found ability to enjoy the peace within, we become less needy for external stimuli and excitement. We can still enjoy a good party or family occasion, but we don't need them in quite the same way.

This increasing sense of self-sufficiency is central to the benefits that will start to grow as we continue meditating. As we've seen stress comes from many directions, triggered by real or imaginary situations and events. But one of the main drivers is our subconscious focus on achievement in one way or another. At work, in relationships and elsewhere in our lives.

Once we realise that the only true achievement is to generate real peace inside our mind and being, we can start to relax. It's not that we won't want to continue succeeding, it's just that the whole process will take on a new perspective. Our daily meditation automatically shows us what we are truly capable of, which doesn't rely on anyone or anything else. It's very liberating in many different ways.

This new found liberty comes from understanding that every moment has the chance to delight us, if only we let it. When we sit in meditation, we learn how precious each moment is, in a very real sense. When we start meditating we may be frustrated at what we perceive as a lack of progress (we want peace, and we want it now!), but over time we will start to appreciate that it is having an effect on us, even if it's happening more gently than we expected.

Because of this, we can start to appreciate the gentler process of life, away from the artificiality of modern day demands. A tree doesn't grow any faster because you want it to, it grows according to nature's laws. In the same way our lives don't have to be constantly yoked to the demands of some illusory material goal. We can take time to enjoy each task, each achievement and each small triumph even if it involves nothing more than washing the dishes. Sound fanciful? You'll see. Over the weeks and months your meditation will slowly bring your life into focus, moment to moment. Instead of stressing about something that won't happen for months, or may never happen, you'll turn your attention to enjoying the moment as it happens now. And when you do that, you start to live properly.

## *Weekly Log*

*Keep a simple log of your week's activities and give yourself 5 points a day for every day when you manage two or more episodes of centered focus on a task or situation. Give yourself 50 points if you manage it every day of the week.*

## * Week five – Detach

*Goal: To spend the week watching our life through a lens of genial dispassion.*

There is no question that one of the most effective stress fighting techniques is to step back from a situation or event and look at it as dispassionately as possible. As we've said before, this can be nigh on impossible when the situation is so traumatic that we are literally shocked into a stupor, but over time, even the most horrendous situation will resolve into some sort of perspective that we can deal with. The trick is to try and take advantage of this point and allow ourselves to realise exactly what we have faced or are facing and how we can deal with it effectively. Again one of the prime movers of this approach is the silence we achieve through our meditation, which over time will build into a generally more peaceful disposition which can cope much more effectively with trauma.

In the interim it can help if we start to look at life events around us generally in a more balanced way. The impact of any event we encounter in life depends completely on how we deal with it internally. For example not many people get upset if they run out of milk, but for others, who may have an obsessive need to maintain order in their home at all times, running out of anything basic can be traumatic. Our goal is to try and stay calm and detached no matter how severe the impacts of daily events are on our emotional and mental processes. By cultivating this kind of placid mental attitude through meditation, we can overcome the potential stress involved in our day to day activities, no matter what form they take.

The object of this week's exercise is to practise watching the events as they occur in our life as if from a distance, in order to strengthen our sense of perspective over problems and issues. This idea of perspective is something that will also come naturally from the practise of meditation, because we will benefit from the growing understanding of our emotional and psychological make-up, and so see where we might be vulnerable to trauma.

In other words, if we start to realise through meditation that we are vulnerable to bouts of anger for no reason, in the most trivial of situations, then we can start to stand back and watch ourselves as these bouts occur, and in what situations. From this we can get a picture of our emotional triggers, and after a while we will be able to dispassionately handle any potential trouble spots or even avoid them completely, simply through our improved self-awareness. This idea of '*the watcher observing the watcher*' is a core aspect of the ancient Far Eastern teachings, in that it is associated with the kind of ultimate wisdom that true gurus exhibit once they become more spiritually enlightened. We can use this detached witness attitude to keep the worst feelings of stress under some sort of control, and as long as we continue with the meditation this exercise can prove very effective in the long term.

One important thing to remember is that a detached attitude is not the same as an uncaring or unfeeling approach. In the latter cases, we are actually just suppressing the feelings we have, which is neither desirable nor healthy. True detachment also includes a core of open hearted compassion, where our emotions are still fully engaged, but we are able to see the whole situation as just a natural part of life, and something which will help us grow in the long run.

By maintaining this compassionate attitude we actually are much more able to cope with life events, because we are not overcome and impeded by our emotional response. This can be incredibly important when we are faced with family trauma, such as the death of a relative, where it is vital that the family pulls together and remains effective in the face of the tragedy. Some people have a natural ability to dig deep and deliver this coping mechanism, where others cannot. But we can help ourselves to learn how to cope through this exercise.

## How does our meditation help?

As we've seen above, one of the most powerful things the meditation brings to our lives is the sense of perspective in terms of what's important and what's less important. This is what makes us resilient to life's knocks from day to day, and contributes so much to the lowering of our overall stress levels. We know from the research that this is more than just an esoteric effect too. There seems to be some physiological foundation to how the meditation changes the brain, which is instrumental in delivering this kind of mental stability. We may never know the exact causes, but it's enough to know that we will benefit from the process.

This growing ability to '*be a witness*' of our mental state and thought patterns is central to the process of becoming immune to stress over the long term. If we can stay strong and stable, no matter what extremes life throws at us, then we're able to spend our time and energy enjoying more, instead of worrying more. We don't know exactly how this interplay between our mind, emotions and physical body works out, but we should certainly be able to feel how the meditation soothes away unnecessary angst day to day. In fact we can test this directly by deliberately taking no action on something which we would usually deal with in an instant. If instead of acting impulsively we wait until after our next meditation, we may notice that the course of action we were going to take, can be replaced with one which is less stressful and yet more effective. It's as though the meditation has given us an added insight into a more efficient way of living. Try it and see, and log whether it works for you.

## *WEEKLY LOG*
*Keep a simple log of your week's activities and give yourself 5 points if you manage to watch yourself and your reactions two or more times during the week. Give yourself 50 points if you manage it every day of the week.*

## * WEEK SIX - SURRENDER
*Goal: To spend the week surrendered to the flow of our life and desires.*

Surrender is one of the most fundamental aspects of any balanced approach to life. The Buddha is said to have achieved his full state of enlightenment only when he surrendered his search for Nirvana after years of asceticism. The word Islam means surrender, in the sense of bowing down to the divine will. In terms of fighting off stress, it means letting go of the things that we cannot change or affect, in order to obtain inner mental peace.

The idea of surrender is often confused with indolence or nihilism, where we just don't care. But in reality surrender is a state of mind whereby we stay calm even though things are not happening the way we hoped or planned. Often when we take a step back from our plans, we can see them more clearly and refine or abandon them in favour of better solutions. The thing that makes the concept of surrender so difficult for us to adopt is the fact that we're constantly warned that we have to take action or suffer the consequences. 'Strike now, while the iron is hot', 'don't dilly dally' are all examples of the idea that we must maintain control of our destiny and once again, obtain our desired results. There's nothing wrong with being positive of course, so we need to keep striving for outcomes otherwise life is not worth living, but ideally it should be done in a balanced way, and not under some sort of mental duress.

A lot of this comes from our innate human fear of uncertainty. When we feel out of control, or things aren't going according to plan, we face an uncertain future, and this is something that the human psyche finds intolerable. It may be a consequence of us living in the age of logic and reason, but we're not supposed to be uncertain, we're always told to be decisive for this reason.

It's as though uncertainty is a sign of weakness, demonstrating our inability to cope. But in fact we can use the opportunities that an uncertain future offers, by accepting change as a positive force in our lives. We can accept life as it is, not as we necessarily think it should be. At the end of the day we can often benefit hugely from something unexpected popping up when we least expect it, even if it is less than pleasant, because it helps us to introspect, and perhaps make changes to adapt. The object of this week's exercise then is to embrace the idea of letting go of various aspect of our lives, day to day. Are you used to organising your itinerary weeks in advance? Why not try reining it in to just a few days and see how well you cope with being a little more spontaneous? Do you hate the idea of not knowing about something well in advance? Why not surrender and find out at the time what's involved or who's going to be at the party? Surrender the little things to the ether at first, and who knows you may enjoy it.

When we're young we live our lives free from the need to plan and organise and control. We just go with the flow. We don't have much say over our daily program anyway, so we tend to spend time enjoying rather than thinking about things. Why do we have to lose that spontaneity and enjoyment of the moment just because we're getting older? By 'not sweating the little things' we lose a huge chunk of the type of things which cause stress, because they become unimportant in the grand scheme of things. Surrender really is, quixotically, the most liberating experience of all.

#### HOW DOES OUR MEDITATION HELP?

To be surrendered is one of the most difficult things we can try to achieve in life. Especially our modern secular life, which has little time to spend on acknowledging anything like the concept of a cosmic will. It's all a bit cliché and almost ludicrous to many people. But surrender doesn't mean we have to become a fatalist, it means we have to look for a flow of life and adapt to it. The cynics laugh at the idea of a flow of life, and point to man's achievements in science, space and industry as proof that the only flow that counts is the man-made version. But our civilisation is still too young in the grand scheme of things to make a final call on whether we're heading in the right or wrong direction.

We cannot surrender until we accept a form of natural order as a possibility, if not a reality, and meditation gives us a base on which to frame that idea. What we experience in meditation may be called esoteric by the cynics, or even delusional, but if it delivers peace, is that wrong? Right now across the world, millions of people meditate every day, trying in their own way to tap into the gentle flow of nature and restore balance to their lives. Are they all wrong?

Our meditation slowly builds up a sense of reality, of importance and perspective which is essential before we can even start to consider surrender. Until we can understand who we really are, and get a grounded view of our existence, it's impossible to accede control from our ego to the flow of some invisible agency. Every day's meditation gives us the context within which we can test out this surrender. We use meditation because we are seeking to improve our mental interaction with the world, and eventually we realise that in order for this to work properly we need to stop thinking (!) that we are responsible for everything that happens in that personal universe. As Hamlet says to Horatio in Act 1, Scene V:

*'There are more things in heaven and earth, Horatio,*
*Than are dreamt of in our philosophy.'*

Through the power of our meditation we start to experience the reality of that statement on a daily basis, but the true significance of those words only really become clear once we remove the mental obstacles we have erected in the name of rationality. There are things we don't understand, and things which we may never understand, such as the nature of consciousness and the mind, but that shouldn't stop us from exploring the more benign aspects of existence through meditation. Once we do, we may find that surrender comes easier to our soul than we could ever imagine. And brings with it more benefits than we could ever dream of.

## WEEKLY LOG

*Keep a simple log of your week's activities and give yourself 5 points a day for every day when you manage two or more episodes where you surrender a task or situation. Give yourself 50 points if you manage it every day of the week.*

## ★ WEEK SEVEN – CHARITY

*Goal: To move our attention away from our own internal struggle to positive external action.*

Now that we're familiar with the meditation and hopefully have some control over our attention and random thoughts, we can try to take another beneficial step which can really help us to move away from our mental history and re-focus on more positive actions to improve our environment. We call this exercise charity, but it doesn't necessarily mean the type of conventional good deed activity that we associate with the word.

This week focuses on moving our attention from our own problems by trying to do something constructive in our life, environment or relationships. The idea is for us to transfer any lingering negative emotional baggage into positive external action, which will again help the mind to refresh itself and decouple from the stressful event or situation which brought us to this point in the beginning. By transferring our attention outwards from our internal problems and dialogue, we help to open up our personality to a wider perspective, rather like opening up the shutters to let the light of a summer morning flood in.

The activity ideally needs to involve some sort of benevolent action for others rather than ourselves, but it doesn't mean you have to join a soup kitchen or clothes charity. It can be something as simple as helping your partner complete a task, or taking some routine off their hands every day or week. Doing a new task for a family member, helping with a neighbour, any kind of small action we can take which results in a benefit for another human being or section of a community. It definitely doesn't have to mean you step outside your comfort zone, so if you feel it's too much, then don't try too hard, just relax and continue with the meditation as you are. Maybe at some point in the future you'll feel more energized to act.

Nor does it have to involve you dealing directly with people, if your particular stressor is still too painful for you to cope with at the time. In these cases, anonymous help (even some action over the Internet or via email or something similar?) can have the same effect. It makes you look outwards instead of inwards, and so gives your mind an opportunity to change thinking patterns.

## How does our meditation help?

Every time we sit down to meditate we refresh and energize the spiritual energies inside of us, and these flows work to cleanse out the negative baggage that we have accumulated over the years, and in fact collect every day just by living the modern life. The reason the meditation is so effective at helping us overcome the pain of stressful situations and events is because it has the power not only to deliver the thoughtless awareness, but also to reinvigorate our emotional and psychological side as well.

What this means is we start to rediscover the joy of living, our youthful exuberance and the compassion we may have lost through circumstances. In its own gentle and yet steady way, the meditation gradually restores our humanity. Because of this we can experience a real sense of satisfaction when we start to look around and see how we can help others. Our mental state becomes much more robust, and we gain the confidence we may have lost through our situation.

Of course there's no specific timetable for these kinds of subtle changes in our life, it happens differently for every person, and to a more or less intense degree. However, it's a fundamental part of the overall benefit that comes from the regular practice of meditation and so you should definitely look out for it as you progress through the weeks, months and years.

## Weekly Log
*Keep a simple log of your week's activities and give yourself 10 points for every activity or task you manage to do for someone else in your social circle or environment. The size of the task doesn't matter, just the action. Give yourself 50 points if you manage more than 3 in the week.*

## How did you score?
So it's just a game, but it should be interesting to see how you've scored after seven weeks of this new approach to your mental well-being.

*If you've scored 200 or more* – well done, you're clearly well on your way to achieving a stress free existence, and hopefully a more positive, calm and enjoyable life. Keep it up and don't slack off.

*If you've scored 150 or more* – you're definitely taking it seriously, so great work. Take a look where you're finding it difficult and see how you can improve things a little.

*If you've scored 90 or more* – well there's definitely room for improvement, but you're still on the right track. Remember it's not a race, so you've got plenty of time to relax and let your life take a more balanced turn for the better.

*If you scored 50 or more* – Perhaps you need a little more encouragement to focus effort on yourself right now? If you want to get something out of the program, why not devote a bit more space in your life to your mental well-being to help it along? Don't give up though!

The tasks and points on this fun exercise are designed to help us maximize the fruits from the meditation, while at the same time giving us context and feedback for the process we are undertaking. If we can keep our attention focused on the important things in our life, and use the meditation to learn perspective, then we can start to dissolve the mental barriers we erect and start to enjoy life as it is meant to be lived. Use the points system to keep track of your progress, but in a light hearted way. It's not designed to be an exam or test, it's there to help you exercise your mental and spiritual powers in order to improve and strengthen them. There's no reason why you can't continue to use them for as long as you feel they help, and it may even be a great way to keep a diary of your progress over many years, until you feel the system has outlived its usefulness.

The main thing is to enjoy your meditation, and enjoy the process you are undertaking. If done with an open heart and mind, it can change your life, so give it the chance and see whether there is a grain of truth residing deep within your being.

## References
1. http://en.wikipedia.org/wiki/Slow_Movement
2. http://new.ted.com/talks/ric_elias
3. http://jamesclear.com/marginal-gains
4. http://en.wikipedia.org/wiki/Flow_(psychology)

# NOTES

# NOTES

# - CONCLUSION -

There is no simple answer to the problems of stress. There are palliatives peddled on every street corner, ranging from pills to positive thinking, but at the end of the day almost all of these solutions will only offer a temporary respite from the symptoms of stressful thinking. The core problem lies in the fact that we inhabit a space in our mind which is extremely stubborn and resistant to change. The result is we can find it extremely difficult, if not impossible, to alter our core behaviours, even when we're suffering through a stressful set of circumstances. And so we bounce from remedy to remedy, cure to cure, trying to find something, anything which will help us escape from the constant barrage of negative thoughts and attitudes that cause the pain.

I'm confident, however, that by following the guidance given in this book, you'll be taking an important step towards finding a new and invigorating oasis of peace you can use at will. By following the meditation program outlined here, you will be taking crucial action to regain control over your life and not be dominated by any problems you may be facing. But even so, as with starting a new diet, the level of benefit you receive from your practice will depend very much on how well you sustain your efforts.

As I mentioned in the introduction, it is essential that you try and maintain your meditation regularly every day in order to benefit from the changes that come from experiencing the silence in thoughtless awareness. Because this silence is what delivers the fundamental changes to your life and attitudes, dissolves the stress you are experiencing and helps you effectively avoid stressful situations in the future. The wonderful thing is you have everything on hand already, you don't need any external items to make it all work. You will also be sharing in an experience that hundreds of thousands of others across the world also enjoy every day, enriching their lives with regular thoughtless awareness.

It's quite astounding just how beautifully made this collection of cosmic waves and particles we know as the universe is, and how elegantly the human body and mind work together to translate it all. What's even more amazing is how easy it can be for each of us to manipulate the mental universe we inhabit. Our mind can make it a place of light and laughter, or a dungeon, and it is up to us to work out which way we wish to go. Even in the face of the most dire circumstances and events, we hope you've learned that you don't have to trudge down the dark corridor if you don't want to. You can choose to use the power you have deep inside you to turn the darkness into light.

The important thing to remember is the real agent of change is the Kundalini energy, which helps your meditation work as effectively as it does. You don't have to buy it over the counter, or queue up for an appointment. Any time you need to tap into the peace inside your mind, you'll find it's there waiting for your summons. Free of charge. The Kundalini is an incredible part of us all, and even if there are no instruments which exist yet to measure its effects, we can still experience the benefits of the meditation every time we sit down and allow this benign force to work.

It's not a trivial journey because it does require commitment, but what we do know is every one of us, without exception, has all the tools we need to take action and find the light. We may not completely understand the process, any more than we understand where our consciousness comes from, but that doesn't mean it's not giving us what we need, when we need it. So why not just lie back and relax, and allow our natural buoyancy and the salt water to help us float along with the gently flowing ocean tides? If you find that the meditation gives you the kind of peace you've been looking for, then you'll know it works, and it's all yours. In a similar vein, we should understand that the peace we discover within ourselves during this journey is a treasure we should cherish. Love it, appreciate it, desire it with all your heart, and don't let it slip away because you feel overwhelmed by mundane issues or incidents in your life. It's more precious than you can ever imagine!

Nowadays it can be fashionable to dismiss this type of joyful journey as random or even self indulgent, when in fact it is nothing less than your well deserved reward for taking time to focus on your inner being with an open heart and mind. But be resolute. Don't stop meditating just because you get the flu, or it's Christmas and the family is over, or your favourite aunt just died or any of a thousand other reasons which may come up. Use these life events to spur you to even greater efforts to locate the peace inside yourself, because it will still be there, no matter what crazy stuff is happening in your environment. Almost everyone who travels this road has to navigate over bumps and cracks, sometimes for longer than would seem reasonable. But if your desire is strong enough, you'll pass over them, at which point you'll be able to look back and wonder what all the fuss was about.

Remember this one crucial fact. You may not have control over every event that occurs in your life, the ups, the downs, the tragedies, triumphs and comedies. But you do have control over what steps you take to enjoy your existence, become a better person and extract the maximum you can from your life, no matter what the circumstances. And the very foundation stone of that control will come from the power of your regular episodes of thoughtless awareness.

It is these precious periods in meditation which make the difference between merely using mental exercises to try and think yourself better, and actually conducting the subtle micro-surgery on your mind that has the power to change your life. The human mind is the most amazing item in the universe, because it is the universe. It does everything for us, on every level. It creates our reality and shapes our experiences. By using the gentle but powerful meditation in this book, you are doing nothing more than bringing your mind and soul into the kind of harmony that is the destiny of every human on this planet. Godspeed!

NOTES

## NOTES

# - RESOURCES -

### FREE 7 WEEK ONLINE EMAIL COURSE

Our free 7 week online meditation course is delivered to your inbox via email once a week, after you register on the website at www.meditationforstress.net. The course is designed to work alongside this book to help you get the most out of your meditation, as well as provide practical tools such as soothing music to assist your thoughtless awareness.

You can also sign up for the course right here using your smartphone or tablet camera and a barcode reader (see below):

The course is deliberately delivered one part per week so as to keep things progressing at a measured pace, and the content of the course will change as you progress over the weeks. You may unsubscribe from the emails at any time, and if you have any questions, feel free to contact us via email or the contact form available on the website.

Meditation for Stress – www.meditationforstress.net
Sahaja Meditation – www.sahajameditation.com

To browse the references given in each chapter in easy live click links, please visit http://meditationforstress.net/references/. You can also access them with your smartphone by scanning the QR code below with a barcode reader app. For example there is a free one available for Apple, Android and Windows tablet computers and phones at - http://tinyurl.com/barcodeMFS

# - APPENDIX I -

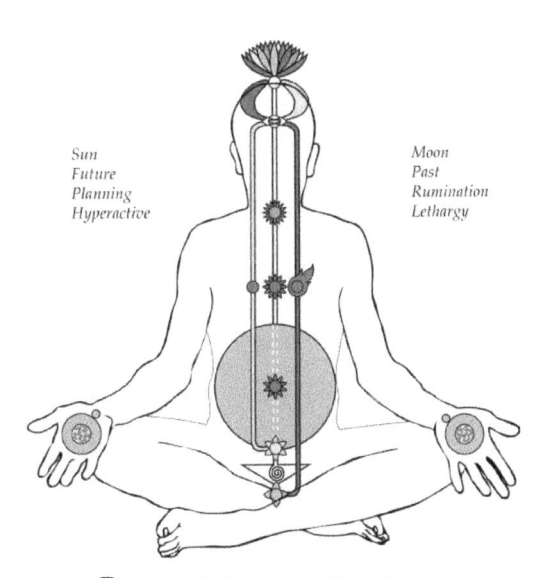

*Sun*
*Future*
*Planning*
*Hyperactive*

*Moon*
*Past*
*Rumination*
*Lethargy*

## Personal Balance checklist

This checklist is designed to help practitioners identify and manage their general state of balance. The core principles of this subject are taken from the Sahaja meditation practice, which is based around the balance and flow of energies inside us all. [1]

This information is useful because it acts as a yardstick to help improve the meditation practice. For example if we are currently going through a particularly hectic period of our life which is generating the stress, then we can identify that we may be in the R State, which represents an imbalance in our right side energies.

This might manifest in something like a general state of irritation, difficulty getting to sleep and other indications as demonstrated below. With this knowledge we can take steps to adjust our activities and perhaps adopt techniques to try and correct the balance, alongside our regular meditation program. The end result should be that our meditations improve, and therefore the process of dealing with our stress is more effective.

We recommend that you try and run through the checklist at the start of every week, and monitor it during the week as much as possible, to keep an eye on how things are developing in general. It's important not to become obsessive about this of course, otherwise that becomes yet another task to add to the stressful issues, but treat it like a temperature gauge which you might refer to now and then when leaving the home.

Over time we learn from experience what our state of balance is anyway, so we will be able to dispense with the formal routine and simply rely on our inner feelings to determine how we're doing. And in general the only time the state of balance becomes a real issue is if it becomes too extreme, and our meditation starts to suffer significantly.

### How to use

To use the checklist, simply refer to the five points outlined below, and see which of these best describe, or are closest to, your experiences at the present time. You should be able to identify a dominant trend from the total of 10 choices (five from each side) given, at which point you can make a decision how mild or severe your particular version is. Once you have determined that, you can then take the actions outlined to try and help your meditation improve, and your state of balance to be restored. As we've said, this is only designed to be a guide, so please don't feel you need to focus on it too much, in fact the most important thing – BY FAR – is to maintain your morning and evening meditation to the best of your ability.

The meditation does all the work in restoring balance, and removing the stress and negative thoughts, everything else is geared to helping that process happen.

**1) Right State** (representing a Right Side Tendency)

★ Typically...
You are a generally positive, outgoing personality, who tends to get on with things and take control whenever necessary. You're always active and making plans for the future, and you get easily irritated with those who don't step into line and keep to the rules. You may find yourself working to exhaustion without realising, until it's almost too late.

★ Extreme...
You can get into a position where you dominate others around you, through pressures of work and stress related issues. This makes it hard for you to get on with people as well as you would like. You get angry a lot, at both small and large things in your life. You are constantly switching between tasks, even though you know you're not doing any of them to the best of your ability.

**Checklist:**
1. Are you having trouble getting to sleep because things keep going around in your mind?
2. Are you finding it hard to get people to do what you need them to do right now?
3. Are you doing too many things at once?
4. Are you making a lot of plans for future events, activities and actions?
5. Are you easily irritated at the moment?

**Results:**
If your checklist results indicate that you are operating more in the Right State (either in general or at this moment), then you may need to adjust your general approach to cool down your sun

side, and restore some balance to your life. This can include taking things slower, avoiding heating situations such as arguments, aggressive activities and excessive judgemental situations. During your meditations use the water and ice techniques to cool down your right side, to restore balance.

Pay attention to the types of food you eat and avoid or cut down significantly on those which can heat up your liver through excessive toxin content (e.g. caffeine, rich fatty foods, alcohol, spicy foods etc). Take regular rest periods (however short) to restrain and reign in your attention. Sit and introspect silently somewhere private every now and then for a few minutes to force this to happen.

**2) Left State** (representing a Left Side Tendency)

★ Typically...
You're a contemplative individual who prefers to make sure they've thought through the implications of every activity before acting. You generally feel less sure about outcomes and you're quite willing to delay action till another day if necessary. You sometimes allow yourself to be controlled in relationships and feel guilty for problems that can occur.

★ Extreme...
You can find yourself feeling very vulnerable or guilty for no real reason at all, either with work colleagues, friends or family. Sometimes when you're in a low mood – which happens quite often at times – you can feel you're a victim, alone and without any support. At these times you look back on your past life with regrets for what might have been. You find yourself easily sent into a downward emotional spiral, and it's hard to say motivated.

**Checklist:**
1. Are you finding it difficult to get up in the morning, because you feel rather uninspired?

2. Are you not feeling very good about yourself and your life direction right now?

3. Are you feeling a little lonely and isolated sometimes during these days?

4. Are you lacking your usual discipline when it comes to getting things done at the moment?

5. Are people around you are forcing things on to your shoulders without consideration?

**Results:**

If your checklist results indicate that you are operating more in the Left State (either in general or at this moment), then you may need to adjust your general approach to heat up your moon side to restore balance to your life. This can include avoiding dark broody environments as much as possible. If you live or work in such a space, then take as much of an opportunity to counteract it as you can, either by sitting at the window, taking walks in the open air, or keeping your environment well lit at all times.

Maintain a list of goals you want to reach each week, and ensure that you refer to it regularly and force yourself to complete them within the time limits if possible. During your meditations use the techniques for lightening up your left side, with the use of light and heat.

Pay attention to the food you eat, avoid processed carbohydrates such as starchy foods, and try and eat as much healthy proteins as you can. If you find your thoughts straying onto negative issues with your life or relationships, take control of your attention and direct them to the positive aspects. Sit and feel the light of your best moments in your heart, to clear away the grey mist.

### References
1. http://www.meditateforlife.com/nadis-energy-channels.html

# - APPENDIX II -

## Meditation Tips

1

2

3

4

5

6

## Example Meditation Technique

## Silent Affirmations to help us transition into meditation

A useful technique to use during the early days of our meditation practice is to silently say a short set of 'affirmations' at the start of each meditation session. These affirmations help us to take our attention inside and enter into a peaceful zone. We can close our eyes, place the right hand in the indicated locations and silently repeat the statements to ourselves a few times as we slide into thoughtless awareness. *See the illustration above for the relevant hand positions.*

1. Please let me be less anxious
2. Please let me be more detached
3. Please let me be more forgiving
4. Please let me enjoy thoughtless meditation

**Note**
5. We may feel a very gentle coolness at the top of our head during or after meditation.

6. Once we have said the affirmations (above), we can sit silently with our eyes closed and hands resting lightly on our laps during the remainder of the session.

# NOTES

# - APPENDIX III -

## MEDITATION TO IMPROVE SLEEP

One of the first things to suffer when we become stressed is a regular good night's sleep. This is mostly because we can't switch off, so the minute our head hits the pillow we find our minds racing with unwanted thoughts. It also doesn't help that most of us typically spend our days consuming significant amounts of caffeine laden coffee and tea, as well as alcohol, and exercise our minds with late night television or Internet browsing, all of which can adversely affect how well or badly we sleep.

As with many other aspects of our deeper psychological and physical well-being, we still don't have all the answers about sleep, and why we appear to need to spend a third of our lives asleep. Scientists have developed theories[1], or course, including the fact that it seems the body does most of its rejuvenation work while we sleep[2]. Activities such as muscle growth, tissue repair and protein synthesis occur mostly, or in some cases only, while we are asleep.

We know also that sleep deprivation can have drastic effects on our physiology, including death and severe ill health.[3] Animals deprived of sleep for long enough lose their immune function completely and die in a matter of weeks.[4] Our bodies enter into an anabolic state while we sleep, which is when most of the repair and rebuilding of our system occurs. During the day when we're awake our body is engaged in the production and use of energy via catabolism.[5] The whole subject is further clouded by the fact that it's not just the act of sleeping that's important, but also the quality of our sleep. It seems as if, of the four main stages of sleep that have been identified so far, REM and Stage 3 NREM are vital to our well-being, and if they are degraded significantly we start to suffer all manner of physical and mental ailments. REM (or rapid eye movement) sleep is light sleep which appears to encourage dreaming, while Stage 3 NREM (non-rapid eye moment) is truly deep sleep.[6]

The damage to our general sleep patterns caused by stress, along with the concomitant daily use of stimulants such as caffeine and even basic issues associated with ageing, mean that we can easily enter into a steady vicious cycle of degraded sleep leading to impaired waking performance, which in turn increases the level of our stress. As with all such cycles, it needs to be broken if the stress is to be reduced in our lives. Again, because we know that the most vulnerable part of our sleep pattern is generally the first stage (where we are trying to 'fall' asleep) and which is typically being blocked by racing thoughts, we can probably realise that anything which improves this stage should also benefit the other 3 stages in turn. And this is where meditation comes into play.

## MEDITATION TO HELP SLEEP

There are two crucial benefits for our sleeping patterns which come from a regular practise of meditation. The first is the slow reduction in the pace and patterns of thoughts that come from learning how to achieve thoughtless awareness. This is especially important with the short evening meditation, which serves to remove the excitable aspects of our day through silent introspection. By taking the time to allow our mind to settle down again after the exertions of the day, we move ourselves into a perfect state to transition to the initial NREM Stage 1.

This is the time when our head hits the pillow, and we're in that place between sleep and wakefulness. This is the point at which we are most vulnerable to racing thoughts, and this is typically the time when all the tossing and turning occurs as our thoughts prevent us from falling into a more sustained state of sleep. By meditating before we go to bed, we can help those thoughts to slow down, and so once we reach the bed, we are not so prone to mental noise. We may still think, but the pattern is gentler, and therefore we can slide more easily into a deeper sleeping state.

#### Useful Tip

One of the techniques we can use alongside our evening meditation to help us sleep better is something which has been around for ages, but we've largely forgotten in this modern era. The idea of placing the feet in a bowl of warm water to relax has been around for ages,[7] and most of us know how relaxed we feel if we have a nice hot bath before bedtime, so it should come as no surprise that we can use the same principle with our evening meditation to remove hectic thoughts and relax more easily.

To do an evening footsoak meditation, all we need to do is run some warm water into a suitable utensil (typically a washing up sized bowl), throw in a small handful of cooking salt, and sit with our feet in the bowl as we meditate. We don't have to do this for long, maybe 10 to 15 minutes, but the effects should be significant. This simple technique serves to suck out all the tension of the day, and leave us feeling deliciously relaxed and ready for a good night's sleep.

Once we have finished the meditation, we can rinse and dry our feet, empty the water down the toilet bowl, and continue with our preparations for bed. We should try to keep the bowl for footsoaking only, for hygiene purposes.

When we eventually head for bed we can continue the treatment by maintaining our meditative mood, and as we settle down for the night, we should not be alarmed if the racing thoughts return, but instead try and control our attention as we do in meditation, to help slow the flow of thoughts. We can do this very simply by taking our attention to the top of our head as we lay in bed, and in fact we can even try using a few of the affirmations we use in our formal meditation practice every day.

In effect we are training our attention to ignore the thoughts, and instead to try and transfer us gently into the same kind of peaceful, mentally quiet zone that we achieve during meditation. In this way, we will find it much easier to drift off to sleep gently, even though thoughts may still be flowing through our mind.

The second major benefit from the meditation is the fact that over time our minds become sufficiently quiet so we don't have as many problems getting back to sleep when we inadvertently awake during the night. One of the most debilitating aspects of going through a stressful period is being unable to return to sleep after we wake up, due to the thoughts which start up immediately we reach full consciousness. This is especially true if we've spent a long time trying to get to sleep in the first place.

We move through several different stages of light sleeping during a night, and these periods are when we are most vulnerable to partially waking up as we emerge from deep sleep or REM stages. Normally we barely surface and can slide back into a deeper pattern easily, however stress and anxiety can often brutally interrupt this process, and trigger all the negative thoughts again. After we have been meditating for a while, we become more resilient to this effect, and can more easily return to a more natural and beneficial sleep pattern after slipping through our light sleep stages. Imagine a world where sleeping pills are a thing of the past!

## Conclusion

Sleep deprivation is probably one of the most debilitating things that attends the onset of severe stress, and it has the potential to set up a vicious cycle of increasing anxiety through tiredness and increased depression.[8] There may also be chemical reasons why getting a good night's sleep is so important in fighting stressful episodes, which is why it can be so crucial to take action to improve our chance of enjoying a proper sleeping pattern.[9]

Meditation can definitely help. The slowing of our racing thoughts, the ability to restore our interrupted sleep and the gradual erosion of negative thought patterns over time, all can help us fight the perils of insomnia effectively and without the need for drugs or other artificial aids. The use of the footsoaking technique is also a valuable tool, and one which can provide a surprisingly effective addition to thoughtless awareness in soothing the mental clutter which can impair our sleep patterns so harmfully.

## References

1. http://www.bbc.co.uk/news/health-24567412
2. http://www.bbc.co.uk/news/health-27695144
3. http://healthysleep.med.harvard.edu/healthy/matters/consequences/sleep-and-disease-risk
4. http://healthysleep.med.harvard.edu/healthy/matters/benefits-of-sleep/why-do-we-sleep
5. http://en.wikipedia.org/wiki/Anabolic
6. http://en.wikipedia.org/wiki/Sleep
7. http://www.namas-natural-remedies-for-health.com/natural-sleep-remedies.html
8. http://www.ncbi.nlm.nih.gov/pubmed/16335332
9. http://consumer.healthday.com/encyclopedia/stress-management-37/stress-health-news-640/sleep-deprivation-and-stress-646063.html

NOTES

# - APPENDIX IV -

## PERSONAL STRESS TEST

### PERCEIVED STRESS SCORE - 4

**INSTRUCTIONS**

The questions in this scale ask you about your feelings and thoughts during THE LAST MONTH. In each case, please indicate your response by placing an "X" over the circle representing HOW OFTEN you felt or thought a certain way.

|   | | Never<br>0 | Almost Never<br>1 | Sometimes<br>2 | Fairly Often<br>3 | Very Often<br>4 |
|---|---|---|---|---|---|---|
| 1 | In the last month, how often have you felt that you were un able to control the important things in your life? | ○ | ○ | ○ | ○ | ○ |
| 2 | In the last month, how often have you felt confident about your ability to handle your personal problems? | ○ | ○ | ○ | ○ | ○ |
| 3 | In the last month, how often have you felt that things were going your way? | ○ | ○ | ○ | ○ | ○ |
| 4 | In the last month, how often have you felt difficulties were piling up so high that you could not overcome them? | ○ | ○ | ○ | ○ | ○ |

© Sheldon Cohen - http://www.psy.cmu.edu/~scohen/

The above evaluation is a common way of evaluating your current levels of stress. By answering honestly, and then adding up your scores you will gain a measured idea of how stressed you are at the present time. The maximum stress score for this evaluation is 16 points, so scores above 8 may indicate elevated stress levels.

*[Note: To add up the scores correctly, reverse the question scores for number 2 & 3 ONLY. So for example Never = 4 points, while Very Often = 0 points. The other two questions are scored normally. Then add up all the points you score from the four answers to get your total.]*

NOTES

# - APPENDIX V -

## An Hypothesis of Sahaja Meditation

At its most basic level the universe is composed only of waves and particles. Everything we see, hear, touch, smell and taste has its origin in these waves and particles. It is our mind that does the translation. We already know that this process can take some interesting aspects, as with people who experience synesthesia [1] who can literally 'see' sounds as colours, as well as hear them.

We are able to measure both particles and waves through the use of sophisticated instruments, but we are reaching the limits of our ability to observe some of the smallest, most indeterminate particles and we simply have no way of knowing how much further out the electromagnetic spectrum stretches beyond our present understanding. Scientists know that the EMS is theoretically infinite and continuous, but since we do not have any instruments capable of measuring beyond current extremities, we can only surmise what else may exist outside the observable universe. In fact up until relatively recently, light was the only known part of the spectrum, but in 1800 scientists started discovering new parts of the spectrum starting with infra-red and ultraviolet radiation.[2]

One hundred years later, gamma rays, the highest frequency so far found, were discovered, and there science has stalled, waiting for a breakthrough or improved instrumentation to enable further exploration. With this in mind, there is a case for suggesting an hypothesis which states that the sensations felt in the mind and on the body during a Sahaja meditation may actually be a form of wave which to date has not been able to be measured by any known instrumentation.

## THE MEDITATION EXPERIENCE

Practitioners of Sahaja meditation are familiar with a sensation described as a 'cool breeze' on the hands and also various parts of the body, including the head. This cool sensation has been commonly described as rather like a very subtle, gentle flow of cool wind over the hands or head, which only occurs when the practitioner is in a balanced state of meditation or experiences some sort of spiritual encounter.

The breeze has no connection with the environment, and practitioners have stated that the sensation occurs even in hot environments, with closed windows and no discernible opportunity for a breeze to occur. One practitioner even describes testing the sensation by seeing if it could be felt while having a very hot bath in a small bathroom with no windows or fans, with positive results. There have been several experiments to measure the temperature of the hands during a Sahaja meditation, and the findings have shown that there is a distinct drop in temperature on the surface of the hand during meditation which has no obvious environmental cause. This temperature shift reverts to normal immediately after the meditation stops, and while in the same surroundings, and only re-occurs again when another meditation session or spiritual encounter is initiated.

Despite the temperature anomaly, there is no explanation for the sensation of a gently moving 'breeze' across the hands, and it is because of this that the experience is commonly ascribed as a deeply spiritual one by those who practice the meditation. It is, however, entirely possible that what is actually being experienced is a direct expression of a new form of as yet undiscovered electromagnetic wave, which is flowing because of some sort of unknown access to a new portion of the spectrum by the brain/mind in meditation.

This hypothesis could explain several things.

⋆ It is entirely possible that the mind has the power to tap into physical states which cannot be explained through the usual theories. Experienced meditators regularly report on feelings of bliss, joy or other states. While our current instrumentation may be too blunt or imprecise to measure them, it is possible that these experiences are the result of our mind in meditation tapping into an unknown source of dopamine triggering electromagnetic waves.

⋆ Experienced meditators learn that with practice they can induce these peaceful feelings by channelling their attention to the limbic area at the top of the head, which suggests that the mind can be trained to use neuro-feedback to move beyond conventional alpha and theta waves to a new level of brain wave experience which so far is unmeasurable.

⋆ Experienced Sahaja meditators are also able to work with these 'vibrations' as they are called, to help other people enter into a deeper meditative state, often by doing nothing more than using their hands to encourage the flow of 'energy' optimally around the body. It makes a lot more sense to understand this phenomenon if we accept that they are actually using the balanced state of their brain to connect to and channel these new waves in beneficial ways throughout the body.

⋆ The fact that meditators can also experience vibrational feedback from inanimate objects as well as people, even across vast distances, suggests that these vibrations exhibit a typical range and penetration which can't be found with some of the measurable electromagnetic waves.

⋆ It is possible that we are actually all 'swimming' in these waves, but it is only those whose brains have been 'tuned' or 'connected' to the frequency in some way which can tap into the experience. Sahaja meditation makes frequent reference to a crucial energy called the Kundalini, which appears to be the catalyst which makes this effect happen in the first place.

★ If this hypothesis is correct, it should be possible for any connected person to help another person become connected simply by activating the catalyst Kundalini with the already connected attention of their mind. In fact this is the reality. This method of passing it on can happen over huge distances, over a telephone, via a computer screen or any other remote method available.

★ While it may appear to be wild conjecture as to the exact nature of these 'waves' or experiences, it is clear that there is some crossover between an indeterminate and yet very real experience of 'coolness' and some sort of natural phenomenon which is as yet unmeasurable, but only experiential. There is precedent with other forms of electromagnetic radiation which have been measured only subsequently to being discovered through experimentation (see William Hershel and infra-red). The concept of this new realm of radiation, if eventually proven through scientific measurement, may also explain additional phenomena which currently have no home in the applied physics arena. Things like collective consciousness, spiritual experiences and aspects of holistic health such as Homoeopathy currently sit uneasily with all but the most open-minded scientists.

## CONCLUSION

The above hypothesis is of course highly speculative, and I present it here only as an example of the kind of theories which could explain those aspects of our 'reality' which can seem esoteric. We currently have no way of knowing if this theory or any other theory could possibly be correct, because we have no instruments capable of doing the necessary measurements, however who knows, perhaps one day...? If a genuinely logical approach to the whole idea of a vastly larger spectrum were to be adopted, there might be an impetus to try and deliver measurable scientific results to back up the experiential claims of authentic esoteric practitioners the world over.

## REFERENCES
1. http://en.wikipedia.org/wiki/Synesthesia
2. http://en.wikipedia.org/wiki/Electromagnetic_spectrum

# NOTES

# - KNOWLEDGE? -

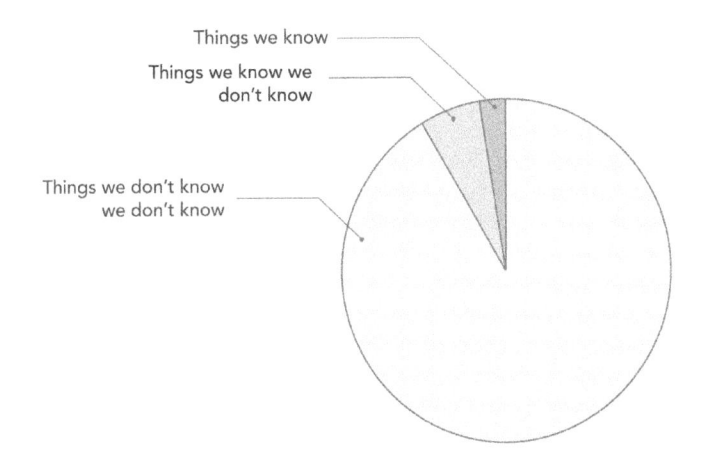

Things we know

Things we know we don't know

Things we don't know we don't know

## Weekly Progress Notes

It can help in the early days if you keep track of your progress as it happens, in whichever way suits you best. Below is a basic template you can use if you wish.

* Meditation. Tick off once or twice each day as applicable
* Silence? Did you experience any episodes of thoughtless awareness during the meditation?
* The Day? Overall has it been a good or bad day (score out of 10 perhaps, with 1 being bad and 10 being great)?

**Week One**

|  | Mon | Tue | Wed | Thu | Fri | Sat | Sun |
|---|---|---|---|---|---|---|---|
| Meditation |  |  |  |  |  |  |  |
| Silence? |  |  |  |  |  |  |  |
| The Day? (Good/Bad?) |  |  |  |  |  |  |  |

**Week Two**

|  | Mon | Tue | Wed | Thu | Fri | Sat | Sun |
|---|---|---|---|---|---|---|---|
| Meditation |  |  |  |  |  |  |  |
| Silence? |  |  |  |  |  |  |  |
| The Day? (Good/Bad?) |  |  |  |  |  |  |  |

# PROGRESS NOTES

## Weekly Progress Notes

### Week Three

|  | Mon | Tue | Wed | Thu | Fri | Sat | Sun |
|---|---|---|---|---|---|---|---|
| Meditation |  |  |  |  |  |  |  |
| Silence? |  |  |  |  |  |  |  |
| The Day? (Good/Bad?) |  |  |  |  |  |  |  |

### Week Four

|  | Mon | Tue | Wed | Thu | Fri | Sat | Sun |
|---|---|---|---|---|---|---|---|
| Meditation |  |  |  |  |  |  |  |
| Silence? |  |  |  |  |  |  |  |
| The Day? (Good/Bad?) |  |  |  |  |  |  |  |

PROGRESS NOTES

## WEEKLY PROGRESS NOTES

### Week Five

|  | Mon | Tue | Wed | Thu | Fri | Sat | Sun |
|---|---|---|---|---|---|---|---|
| Meditation | | | | | | | |
| Silence? | | | | | | | |
| The Day? (Good/Bad?) | | | | | | | |

### Week Six

|  | Mon | Tue | Wed | Thu | Fri | Sat | Sun |
|---|---|---|---|---|---|---|---|
| Meditation | | | | | | | |
| Silence? | | | | | | | |
| The Day? (Good/Bad?) | | | | | | | |

### Week Seven

|  | Mon | Tue | Wed | Thu | Fri | Sat | Sun |
|---|---|---|---|---|---|---|---|
| Meditation | | | | | | | |
| Silence? | | | | | | | |
| The Day? (Good/Bad?) | | | | | | | |

# PROGRESS NOTES

# NOTES

NOTES

Ingram Content Group UK Ltd.
Milton Keynes UK
UKHW042138120523
421633UK00012B/75

9 780954 851910